T0381118

The Golden
Eight-Petaled Lotus
Way of Health and Happiness

Book One

Wisdom, Compassion, and Awakening

Through Mindfulness and Insight Meditation

Lama Losang

BALBOA.PRESS
A DIVISION OF HAY HOUSE

Balboa Press books may be ordered through booksellers or by contacting:

Balboa Press
A Division of Hay House
1663 Liberty Drive
Bloomington, IN 47403
www.balboapress.com
844-682-1282

Cover illustration and design by Joon Thomas.

Print information available on the last page.

ISBN: 979-8-7652-4656-6 (sc)
ISBN: 979-8-7652-4657-3 (hc)
ISBN: 979-8-7652-4655-9 (e)

Library of Congress Control Number: 2023920579

Balboa Press rev. date: 02/23/2024

*To my parents, Nelson and Jeanne Bole, Dharma teacher Khenpo
Karthar Rinpoche, and all the other outstanding teachers mentioned
in this book who have been mentors and guides. I am grateful for the
kindness and generosity of all my teachers and the wisdom and patience
they showed me in demonstrating how to be a better human being.*

Contents

Foreword

We all want to be better people. And despite what people say about this wish—that it's a fool's errand or that it comes from a nagging and perhaps unhealthy self-doubt—there is incredible truth and power in this wish. Yet somehow, beneath all our annoying failings and daily life struggles, we know there's more inside us—more to be seen, more to be known, more to be loved. The source of this wish, according to the ancient teachings of Buddhism, is very simple—it's our Buddha-nature, the mind's natural capacity for goodness, warmth, kindness, and deep insight.

Most of us travel through life without knowing the existence of this deep well of inner clarity and goodness. We might catch glimpses and glimmers through our ability to be awed by a sunrise or art or music, as well as our ability to be touched by gestures of kindness and heroism displayed by others. But the presence and power of this, our most basic nature, remains hidden for many of us. This is where the power of positive connection, called *tendrel* by Tibetan Buddhists, comes into play. According to the teachings of the Buddha, we have encountered both positive and negative people and situations in our myriad lifetimes and depending on our appreciation for these people and situations, our future karma is influenced.

If we see a positive person and receive advice from them and then treasure and follow that advice, we will have a positive connection with that person that can span a whole lifetime or, if you believe in past and future lives, many lifetimes. Such teachers give us the instructions and practices that will allow us to cut through our negative habits and mistaken delusions about ourselves and the world and help us uncover all the positive qualities of love, compassion, and wisdom that are inherent in each of us.

You hold in your hands an example of *tendrel* in action. You picked up this book, perhaps because of the intriguing title, perhaps because of the beautiful cover, not knowing it contains deep teachings that will introduce you to your mind's inner Buddha-nature and inspire you to practice methods to nurture and ripen it.

You also may not know that this book was written by a unique person trained in two spiritual and psychological disciplines, Eastern and Western, who is, therefore, uniquely equipped to explain the teachings on the nature of your mind. But now that you have picked up this book, perhaps you could give it a read and allow *tendrel* to expand your outer and inner horizons.

Lama Losang (David Bole) was born in America but met singular teachers all over the world, including a respected martial artist, a groundbreaking acupuncturist, and a Tibetan master who escaped violent repression in his homeland to give the gift of Buddhist teachings to thousands of fortunate disciples in every part of the globe. Guided by a powerful curiosity born of his own *tendrel* and a fierce determination to learn, Lama Losang overcame obstacles to his educational and spiritual goals and accomplished them one by one. He became a trained psychologist, a gifted healer, and a Tibetan Buddhist teacher.

Having lived as a husband and father and as a second-career monastic in the modern world, Lama Losang is uniquely positioned to know outer and inner aspects of that life and how we might safely navigate them toward better physical and spiritual health. Beyond that, he has shared generously his knowledge, care, and time with students of both the healing arts and spiritual life, "paying forward" what he gained from his own masters. As one of Lama Losang's friends in the Dharma, I've had the benefit of his expertise and appreciate his skill as a healer, communicator, and counselor.

His Golden Eight-Petaled Lotus of Healing classes have inspired many and now has given birth to this book series, which begins with his overview of the meditative path that was taken by ancient masters and now is available to all of us wherever we are—the living room, the coffee shop, the classroom, the hospital. The volume you now hold in your hands contains time-tested methods for developing and accomplishing all these qualities. It is a fitting beginning for Lama Losang's Golden Eight-Petaled Lotus Way of Health and Happiness series and can stand on its own as a primer for anyone interested in pursuing Tibetan Buddhist study and practice.

Ancient Tibetan medical texts describe the following qualities that must be developed before a person can become a healer or teacher like Lama Losang. Those wishing to help others in this way must display:

1. intelligence,
2. compassionate heart,
3. pure intention,
4. skillfulness,
5. diligence, and
6. social ethics.

You'll likely agree that these qualities aren't just needed by physicians and spiritual teachers; they're also important for every person who wants to open their hearts and lives to others, who are all of us.

As our teacher Khenpo Karthar Rinpoche once said, when we first start in the spiritual life, our Buddha-nature may not yet be discovered or developed, but it remains a positive guiding force in our life, in the background of our thinking, nudging us ever closer to the studies and practices that will help us discover and nurture our inner potential. "Your inner wisdom has led you here," he would say to those who attended his early Dharma lectures. "Why don't you stay and see what these teachings have to offer to you?"

You hold in your hand an example of *tendrel* in action. Your inner wisdom brought you here; let's read on and see what these teachings have to offer!

Lama Kathy Wesley
(June 9, 2023)

Acknowledgments

There are many people I wish to thank, who helped me over the years and made this book possible. Special thanks to *Joy Bole*, who has been an excellent partner, teacher, colleague, and friend for over forty years. Her kindness and care for me literally saved my life.

I wish to thank *Jennifer Grant* for initially insisting that this book be published and helping initiate this project.

Thanks to my friend and fellow writer and teacher *Bill Alexander*, who wrote the back cover. We presented many workshops together in the Recovery Community.

A special thanks to *Sibyl Christie* for coming to my rescue with help in creating the graphics, editorial expertise, and her patience in tutoring me in navigating the perplexing problems experienced in a digital world. She was with me from start to finish of this book, and her help was indispensable.

Also, thanks to *Matthew Daley* for his skills in design and unwavering support for this project.

A heartfelt thank you to *Lama Kathy Wesley* for her sage advice and insight over many years of friendship. I Thank her, too, for her kindness and for the inspirational Foreword to this book!

Most importantly, I am grateful to my teacher and spiritual guide, *Khenpo Karthar Rinpoche,* who showed great kindness and confidence in me. Without his guidance, my life would lack the many positive qualities discussed in this book, which he tirelessly taught and demonstrated to his students around the world.

Last, I wish to acknowledge *all my teachers, students, patients, and friends,* who constantly inspire me to never stop learning.

May it benefit all beings!

Introduction

You might wonder how I came to write this book on mindfulness and meditation. The answer to that question is this introduction. I am reminded of *Meetings with Remarkable Men*, a book by the Russian philosopher, mystic, and spiritual teacher George Ivanovich Gurdjieff (1866–1949). This book and the ones to follow are my experiences of "meetings with remarkable men." Here, you will find timeless wisdom of the ages blended with the profound knowledge and understanding of outstanding teachers I had the good fortune to encounter. They also generously shared their experiences and compassionate hearts with me, which, in turn, I am sharing with you.

The Golden Eight-Petaled Lotus, Book 1: Wisdom, Compassion, and Awakening and other books in this series will be somewhat autobiographical. They are based on experiences with many excellent teachers on my continuing journey.

This journey began with my birth in Detroit, Michigan, on July 26, 1949. I was the only child of Nelson and Jeanne Bole, who named me David Nelson. David was after my father's beloved brother (David means "beloved"), and Nelson was my father's name. They had me late in life, in their mid-forties.

I remember growing up in a neighborhood where everyone knew one another, and there was a feeling of community. Because my mother's faith was very strong, she made sure I went to a Catholic school and attended those services regularly. She was raised in a convent following her mother's death shortly after her birth and was placed with the nuns because of her father's ill health and inability to look after her and her two elder sisters. She was cared for by Catholic nuns in a nunnery in San Bernadino, California. Mother developed her deep, abiding faith during her formative years there, which would nourish, guide, and support her throughout her life.

She strongly influenced my education and arranged for me to attend Catholic school from kindergarten to high school. My father left my religious training to my mother. Like many men in those days, he spent most of his time at work. Since my father left early and returned late, my mother and I naturally spent more time together. Through her example, she taught me how to be a good and caring person.

We moved from Michigan to Florida when I was eight years old because of my father's poor health. My mother saw to it that I continued to attend Catholic schools and daily mass. I was an altar boy and enjoyed mass and the solemn chanting of the call and response of the prayers in Latin with the priest. I also appreciated and enjoyed the sacramental rituals, wearing the sacred and devotional vestments, the incense and bells, and other offerings used in the daily mass. I marinated in this environment for many years, being groomed for priesthood. This training would be a meaningful segue to my Buddhist studies and practices that culminated in my becoming a fully ordained Bhikshu, a Buddhist monk, many years later.

I loved Florida. We lived on a small lake, and I enjoyed the wildlife, boating, fishing, nearby ocean beaches, and fantastic weather that was a welcomed change from the long and dreary winters in Detroit. My mother worked as a private-duty registered nurse (RN), and we would frequently go to the beach after she finished her 11:00 p.m.–7:00 a.m. shift. Going to the beach was great! I always returned with some treasure, usually a few beautiful shells to add to my collection.

My mother must have been a superb nurse because she was the night nurse for Joe Kennedy, the father of then-president John F. Kennedy. I would go with my dad to pick her up at the Kennedy compound in Palm Beach when she finished her shift. She even accompanied Joe when he visited his son at the White House! I still have my mother's letters written to me on the White House stationery when she was staying there.

In high school, I began taking classes in martial arts. This interest also led to studies in meditation. I feel this was a continuation of interests cultivated over many previous lives. Two essential tenets in many religions, including Buddhism, are those on karma and reincarnation. These tenets state that we do not come into this world "tabula rasa" or as a "blank slate," as some Western philosophers profess. In the Buddhist view, at birth, we bear the karmic seeds of many past lives. These seeds from our experiences eventually ripen to propel us in specific directions and influence our life choices. We display these predispositions throughout our lives as our various likes, dislikes, talents, and attributes. Every experience leaves its indelible karmic imprint in our minds. These experiences are stored in our mind (Alaya Consciousness) and influence our decisions and actions on our journey.

The only real failure in life is not being true to the truth that one knows.

~ Buddha Shakyamuni

Throughout high school, I participated in team sports, including football and track, becoming the first freshman in our high school to earn a varsity letter in track.

I continued martial arts training at our local YMCA, where I studied a Japanese style of karate called *Renbukan*. These classes were very strenuous and required discipline, attention, and focus. My instructor, Kenji Nonin, was a young Japanese black belt, who inspired and motivated me. He was my role model, and I aspired to be just like him. He introduced me to a Japanese style of sitting meditation called Zazen. This experience opened a new area of interest for me, which I continued to pursue and would greatly influence the path my life was about to take.

However, another turning point in my life was about to take place. My mother's death in December of 1966, when I was seventeen, was the catalyst for the next significant change in my life. With this came increasing self-reliance and discipline of another kind, and I soon left home to attend college and live on my own.

My father was trained as a lawyer, and we had planned that I would follow in his footsteps. He planned for me to be an attorney and possibly run for political office, as he thought I would make a fine senator or become a judge like my grandfather. With that in mind, in the autumn of 1969, I started at the University of Florida, in Gainesville, as a political science/pre-law student. While in my first semester, another change in plan was about to take place.

My interest in health and the wonders of the body-mind connection continued in college and in sports, even winning the University of Florida Intramural Tennis Championship! But a new interest was also arising. It was my growing fascination with the workings and power of the mind. Even tennis brought me closer to meditation and taming the mind! I found a book by Timothy Gallwey titled *The Inner Game of Tennis*. It was about the mental state required to deliver peak performance and how to cultivate that state in sports, work, and every aspect of life.

As it turned out, my time as a pre-law student was short-lived. In my first semester, I took an elective psychology class and met a psychology professor, Sidney Jourard. He was an amazing teacher in the new field of humanistic/transpersonal psychology. In this class, my quest for understanding the power of the mind and the study of meditation began to take form. I changed my major to psychology and started in a completely new direction based on the ancient wisdom of the East.

Although Dr. Jourard is no longer with us, his words remain with me. I think he would approve of my endeavor to write this book for the benefit of others and to risk the chance of ridicule or failure. He said in his writing of the book *The Transparent Self* (1971),

> The act of writing bears something in common with the act of love. The writer, at his most productive moments, just flows. He gives himself naked, recording his nakedness in the written word. Herein lies some of the terror which frequently freezes a writer, preventing him from producing. Herein, too, lies some of the courage that must be entailed in letting others learn how one has experienced, or is experiencing the world.

I also participated in a mind-expanding process called the Arica 40 Day Training. I went on to study the Advanced Arica Training with Oscar Ichazo in New York City. The Arica Institute is an esoteric school founded by the mystic Oscar Ichazo (1931–2020). He is another one of those "remarkable men." This began a quest that culminated in my traveling to India to study yoga with B. K. S. Iyengar (1918–2014) in Pune and to the Sivananda Yoga Ashram in the Himalayas on the Ganges River, near Rishikesh. My quest eventually took me around the world, to India, China, Japan, and Tibet.

The study of psychology at the University of Florida also progressed. Unlike our current world, at that time there was very little interest or written information in scientific literature about meditation, and the word "mindfulness" was not common parlance. I used one of the few books available at the time, *The Relaxation Response* by cardiologist Herbert Benson, as the basis for my doctoral dissertation's research model. With that and my experience, I began my research and writing in 1976.

During this period, I also began my study in Tai Chi with Patrick Watson (1935–1992), founder of the School of Tai Chi Chuan (STCC).

More about this in the next book in the Master Series, *Book 2: Tai Chi/ Chi Gong: Exercises for Health and Longevity.*

As part of my doctoral dissertation, a meditation technique was taught to counselors and psychotherapists. In the dissertation, *The Effect of the Relaxation Response on the Positive Personality Characteristics of Paraprofessional Counselors,* I wrote about the cultivation of enhanced positive personality characteristics in mental health counselors and therapists through the practice of meditation. The University of Florida thought it was important and valuable research and chose to publish it. The book can be purchased through the University of Florida Library Press.

Much has changed in psychology and the field of meditation and consciousness since my time in graduate school. I am happy to say that the research results were statistically significant. The psychotherapists participating in the study who meditated, as opposed to the control group who did not, had significantly improved scores in empathy, positive regard, genuineness, and other characteristics associated with self-actualization, and I was awarded the Doctor of Philosophy (PhD) degree.

I took a teaching position at Greenville Technical College in Greenville, South Carolina, as a professor in the psychology department and later became the dean. I taught psychology classes, counseled patients, and taught yoga and meditation. It was during this time that a strong and growing attraction toward studying medicine began to grow. I became increasingly aware of health issues not being addressed with counseling alone and started looking for a more complete and comprehensive system of medicine to deal with the chronic problems my patients were experiencing.

Although I had very little exposure to Asian approaches to health and healing, I was inclined in that direction. Other than seeing the application of acupressure and healing salves and ointments used as "hit medicine" for strains, sprains, and bruising from the trauma of martial arts training, I was unfamiliar with the complete scope of Asian medicine.

After considerable deliberation and a prophetic dream, I decided to go to England and study acupuncture. Outside of China at that time, there was little opportunity to study classic Chinese Medicine. However, there was one school that I applied to and was accepted. In the summer of 1977, I traveled to Oxford, England, and began my three-year study of acupuncture at the College of Traditional Chinese Acupuncture with Dr. J. R. Worsley (1923–2003). He was considered the foremost proponent of the Five-Element approach to this system of medicine. I became one of the fortunate Westerners accepted into this training program. Prof. J. R. Worsley's teachings were compelling and very different from the Western approaches to health and healing. I enthusiastically continued my studies with him and completed the advanced degree in acupuncture in 1982.

Professor Worsley taught me so much in the classroom about the five elements, acupuncture, and classical Chinese medicine. However, it was his penetrating insight into human nature that taught me so much more. With everyone he met, students and patients alike, he demonstrated love, compassion, patience, and understanding. He continually demonstrated the qualities of a Bodhisattva and embodied the timeless wisdom of the sages of the past. He wholeheartedly demonstrated in his teachings and lifestyle how to enhance our longevity, health, and well-being through internal transformation and by following the laws of nature.

With this knowledge, I returned to Florida and began my practice of acupuncture. The State of Florida granted those of us licensed as Acupuncture Physicians permission to offer a student apprenticeship program. Graduation would qualify them to sit for the national exam and licensure in the state. I was grateful to have been chosen to enroll students in a two-year apprenticeship and was soon busy setting up the training program.

I also studied Tibetan medicine with the renowned doctor, Yeshi Dhonden (1927–2019), when he was teaching Buddhist Studies at Amherst College for a few years in the mid-1980s. Dr. Dhonden was a Buddhist monk who was the physician to the 14th Dalai Lama from 1961 to 1980 and the author of a classic book on the subject called *Health Through Balance: An Introduction to Tibetan Medicine* (1986). Traditional Tibetan Medicine (TTM) is based on the teaching of the Buddha. The Buddha's Four Noble Truths are applied through a diagnostic logic to end our experience of suffering in its myriad forms. TTM's understanding is that illness ultimately results from the three mental poisons: delusion, greed, and aversion.

While Dr. Dhonden was at Amherst, I was one of the six students who periodically came from all over the country to study the classic texts and learn from the master. Our training was ongoing from 1983 to 1986, and we met whenever he was available in the small shrine room of Prof. Robert Thurman's home. Dr. Thurman is an author, teacher, and former monk. Dr. Dhonden taught us the basics of diagnosis and treatment. These classes included the complexities of pulse diagnosis, urinalysis, behavior and lifestyle analysis, dietary modification, herbal formulation, and physical therapies. During one of these training sessions, we had a surprise visit and tea with His Holiness the 14th Dalai Lama, Tenzin Gyatso!

Acupuncture was still very new to the West, and I was the first acupuncture practitioner in my city of Gainesville, Florida. As I continued to build a clinical practice, word soon spread about the improved health benefits patients were experiencing from acupuncture treatment and related Five-Element therapies. To my delight, many people who had a positive experience with their acupuncture treatment wanted to learn more.

One of those who benefited from treatment was Joy, a pediatric intensive care nurse. She had severe and almost crippling arthritis. This was a completely different system of medicine from what she had learned in school. Unfortunately, Western medicine had failed to provide relief, and she was getting worse. Joy came to my office as a new patient and experienced immediate relief from her pain and improvements with other chronic problems. She wanted to know more about this "new" system of medicine but had to return to California to be with her family. Joy eventually returned to Florida to enroll in the apprenticeship program to become a licensed Acupuncture Physician.

So why am I talking about Joy? On December 21, 1986, the Winter Solstice, we were married. Although we are no longer married, we still have an excellent relationship. She did become a licensed Acupuncture Physician (A.P.) in Florida and has contributed greatly and positively to my life. The apprenticeship program mentioned above evolved into *The Florida School of Acupuncture and Oriental Medicine*, where we trained students in the Five-Element style of Dr. J. R. Worsley.

In 1987, I was appointed by Gov. Bob Martinez to the Florida Board of Acupuncture and served in that capacity until 1991. It has been a wonderful journey, and I am grateful to have been able to contribute to this noble profession.

All these experiences culminated in my growing appreciation for the teaching of the Buddha. I saw Buddhism as a supreme psychology and the Buddha as the quintessential physician for understanding and taming the mind to end our suffering. This led to my pursuit of the teachings of the Buddha with the acclaimed master of this mind science, Khenpo Karthar Rinpoche (1924–2019).

Khenpo Rinpoche was born in Eastern Tibet. He is recognized as one of the greatest masters of Tibetan Buddhism and revered around the world. I met Khenpo Rinpoche in 1987, when he accepted our invitation to teach at our Dharma Center in Gainesville (*see Appendix C for more about my first meeting with this most remarkable man*). My wife Joy and I were honored to host him in our home for the duration of his stay. At the conclusion of Rinpoche's visit, he gave many of us the Refuge Vows, the formal commitment to follow the path of the Buddha. Those of us who took these vows established the Gainesville Karma Thegsum Choling Center for Buddhist Studies later that year.

For Joy and me, this was the beginning of what would become a very profound relationship with our teacher. Under his tutelage, we continued to grow our Dharma Center, one of many centers established by Khenpo Rinpoche in the United States and around the world.

There are times when we might recognize the importance of a special person in our life, someone with whom we feel a natural connection and affinity. Khenpo Rinpoche was one of these people. In my daily prayers, I still make the aspiration that from lifetime to lifetime, may I never be separated from my kind and compassionate teacher. From this perspective, I feel my current conditions and accomplishments are the result of aspirations made in many past lives.

My studies in Buddhism continued. I came to a point in my life that I had to acknowledge the strong wish to do the Kagyu three-year retreat with Khenpo Rinpoche. Many causes and conditions needed to come together to achieve this goal. Feeling the growing momentum, I discussed this with Joy, who would be left with a great deal of responsibility. She was wonderful and suggested I contact Rinpoche to ask permission to join the next retreat.

When I called the Karme Ling Retreat Center, Rinpoche must have been standing near the phone when the retreat manager, Karma Lodro answered. I asked Karma Lodro to please ask Rinpoche if I may join the upcoming three-year retreat. I could hear him ask the question and Rinpoche's answer. He immediately said "Yes!" but with one additional comment: "Study Tibetan."

Joy and I made the necessary arrangements and thus began the next chapter in our lives.

I entered the retreat in 2000 at the age of fifty and completed it in 2004. I will talk more about the retreat experience in Appendix A. Unexpectedly, while still in retreat, because of unforeseen circumstances, Joy and I were divorced. After the retreat, Rinpoche asked me to direct the activities and teach in the three Florida Karma Thegsum Choling centers (KTCs). I also reestablished the *Traditional Acupuncture Center* for the practice of acupuncture and the *Gainesville Karma Thegsum Choling* Dharma Center.

In November 2008, Rinpoche invited me to go with him and a group of monks and students to Namo Buddha Monastery in Nepal. With the change in my marital status, the wish to take monastic ordination arose. With Rinpoche's permission and blessing, on November 25, 2008, I did take the vows to become a fully ordained *Bhikshu* (monk) with the 9th Khenchen Thrangu Rinpoche at Namo Buddha Monastery in Nepal.

I was given the name Karma Lodro Sangpo. The name *Karma* for our Karma Kagyu Lineage of the Karmapas, and *Lodro Sangpo* which means "Excellent Intelligence." However, Rinpoche always called me *Losang*, a contraction of Lodro Sangpo, translated as "Kind-hearted." The word *Lama* in Tibetan means "teacher" and the Sanskrit word is *Guru*. After the completion of the retreat, Rinpoche granted me the title *Drupay Lama (Retreat Lama)*. Thus, I am known as *Lama Losang*.

I continue to teach Dharma in centers across the country, transitioning from on-site visits to Zoom. At the time of this writing, we are still experiencing the aftermath of the unprecedented spread of a worldwide pandemic that resulted in death, sickness, fear, and anxiety for millions of people around the world. The teachings presented here can help allay the suffering experienced by so many. Understanding and practicing the compassionate teachings of the Buddha have never been more beneficial and relevant than now.

What I will be presenting in this book and continuing with other books in the series, is a profound and effective system of health and healing called the Golden Eight-Petaled Lotus Way of Health and Happiness. The title came from a vivid dream I had several years ago and was the catalyst for this presentation. In the dream, a beautifully decorated hand, holding a large golden eight-petaled lotus, was being extended out to me—much like the graphic representation on the front cover of this book. I understood this gift being offered to represent the fundamental teachings on the eight healing systems common to India, China, Japan, Southeast Asia, and Tibet.

This teaching goes back as far as the first recognized medical text in China, *The Yellow Emperor's Classic of Internal Medicine*. In that text, these teachings were known as the eight branches and written as a dialogue between the Yellow Emperor Huang Di (2697–2597 BCE) and his physician Qi Bo. That text is divided into eight sections, with each section representing a petal of our Golden Eight-Petaled Lotus.

Book One: Wisdom, Compassion, and Awakening is the first book in the series that will cover the eight different areas of study listed below. It provides an organized way of teaching important concepts and related practices. It provides methods for promoting and cultivating wisdom and compassion through mindfulness and meditation. May all beings benefit!

The Golden Eight-Petaled Lotus Way of Health and Happiness Master Series includes:

Book One: Wisdom, Compassion, and Awakening through Mindfulness and Insight Meditation

Book Two: Tai Chi/Chi Gong: Exercises for Health and Longevity

Book Three: Diet and Nutrition: Food as Medicine

Book Four: Acupressure Massage: Thirty-Six Acupoints for Health and Vitality

Book Five: I Ching and Mo Divination: Consulting the Oracle

Book Six: Feng Shui and Astrology: Ancient Tools for Modern Healers

Book Seven: Herbal Medicine: Integrating Plant Medicine for Health and Healing

Book Eight: Law of the Five Elements: Theory and Practice

As expressed throughout Asian cultures for centuries, the above-mentioned studies were considered the most important branches of learning for health and well-being. Emphasis is placed on the importance of these methods for cultivating health and especially wisdom and compassion. They provide the basis for becoming a happy, healthy, and effective human being. Students of the healing arts were required to train in these fundamentals. They remain essential subjects not only for physicians, but for all of us.

A journey of a thousand miles begins with a single step.

~ Lao Tzu

I have used all these methods and can attest to their power and effectiveness. They have the profound ability to transform our thinking and improve the quality of our life. I will share some of my experiences of using these tools and the deep and far-reaching effects they have had on me.

My heartfelt wish is to share what I have learned over these many years to help guide you in how to listen to your inner wisdom. We are all in the process of creating the work of art that is the tapestry of our life. This study that begins with meditation, mindfulness, and awakening will give you practical tools for living your best life and for creating health and happiness for yourself, your family, your friends, and our world.

Walking this path of venerable teachings requires years to master. Nevertheless, there is a saying to keep in mind: "A journey of a thousand miles begins with a single step." This quote is found in the ancient Chinese classic text *Tao Te Ching* and is attributed to the renowned philosopher Lao Tzu. I invite you to take this step with me. I am confident you will find the journey enjoyable, challenging, and tremendously rewarding.

Wisdom, Compassion, and Awakening

---

*Following the Noble Path is like entering a dark room
with a bright light in the hand: the darkness will be cleared
away, and the room will be filled with light.*

~Buddha Shakyamuni

Welcome, Dear Readers!

I would like to begin by expressing my appreciation and happiness in your interest in learning the guidelines for meditation practice in your life. The practices of meditation and mindfulness ultimately lead to the awakening of our mind's true nature of wisdom and compassion. We start our path by establishing the motivation to study these teachings. We must answer the question, *"Who am I?"* Just like the Buddha, we have to answer this question for ourselves.

There is a story about a young reporter at an airport who spots a Buddhist monk and decides to interview him. The reporter asks, "Sir, what would you say is the world's biggest problem? Is it global warming? World hunger? Corruption?"

The monk smiles and replies, "Before I answer, let me ask you something first ... Who are you?"

The reporter agrees and says, "I am a reporter."

"No, that is your profession," says the monk. "Who are you?"

"I'm John Adams," says the young man.

"No, that is your name." He asks again, "Who are you?"

"I am... a human being," he hesitantly replies.

"No, that is your species," says the monk.

This goes on for some time until the young reporter finally says, "Alright, … it appears I don't know who I am!"

Then the monk answers, "This is the world's biggest problem."

In this book we will look at how the Buddha answered this question and at what eventually led him to enlightenment. I emphasize it, because it is the fundamental question that faces each of us. What follows is the ongoing answer to that question on the nature of the self.

An important ingredient for the success of our journey is having a strong motivation to change our life for the better by adopting new positive habits that are the foundation for your future happiness. We can learn to uproot our negative habits and replace them with positive healthy habits. This requires mindfulness. Mindfulness is a way of training to become more aware of your own mind. This is done through the meditation practices we will study. It is a way to end our suffering and attain true happiness.

The following instructions place the emphasis on our direct inner experience in applying the truths revealed by the Buddha. The Buddha is called the Supreme Physician because, in his words, "My teaching is about suffering and the remedy to end it." Its purpose is to diagnose and offer a remedy for our suffering and discontent. His genius was the ability to analyze suffering and then show us how to apply this wisdom as the remedy to achieve our serenity and peace of mind. The Buddha did not come to teach a new religion or convert anyone; he simply welcomed and taught everyone who wished to awaken to deep peace and truth.

Today, people around the world are struggling with the many difficult challenges that our modern life presents, such as health problems, finances, relationships, climate changes, the threat of war, and much more. This has resulted in overwhelming worry, fear, depression, and anxiety at personal, regional, and global levels.

For many, these myriad struggles have led to such things as substance abuse that are reaching epidemic proportions. In recent studies from CDC, it was reported that over 66 million Americans reported binge drinking. In addition, in 2020, National Survey on Drug Use and Health (NSDUH) reports that over 40 million Americans, aged 12 or older, had a substance use disorder (SUD) in the past year. They report these numbers continue to rise annually.

The World Health Organization has reported that over 280 million people on the planet can be classified as clinically depressed! This includes people of all ages – it isn't limited to adults. Sadly, the latest statistics on adolescent health in our country have shown that over 16 percent of this population suffer from depression. Even worse, depression leading to suicide is one of the major causes of death in adolescents, second only to auto accidents.

Although these disturbing numbers are staggering, unfortunately, they are continually rising. We can conclude from this that a method for spiritual healing and awakening is desperately needed. Data has shown a connection between a spiritual orientation and mental health (*see the Bibliography and Recommended Reading section at the end of the book; The Awakened Brain*). Buddhism shows us that we *can* change and learn how to lead happy, fulfilled lives! This is why it has so much relevance and appeal in our modern world and is making such a strong resurgence. Buddhism has spread from India to China, Japan, Tibet, Southeast Asia, and more recently to the West. Despite certain cultural differences, it currently is proving its ability to peacefully transform the lives of over five hundred million people around the world.

This is why despite Buddhism being one of the oldest of the world's religions, it remains as alive and relevant as it was for its earlier followers. Many scholars and adherents to these teachings, including myself, see it more as a mind science and a supreme psychology than as a religion.

Anyone can derive healing benefits in body and mind if Buddha's teachings are applied consistently in daily life. We all want to be happy and don't want to suffer, but we must have the proper motivation and training to progress. Implementing these practices into our busy lives can be daunting, and they are not a quick fix. Time and consistent effort are required to uproot the habitual negative patterns we have been cultivating for years and even lifetimes.

Each petal of our Golden Eight-Petaled Lotus represents an effective means to cultivate virtue and uproot our negative tendencies, starting with the mindfulness and meditation practices. These methods can skillfully lead us to a solution for the many challenges we are facing.

With each of the eight healing traditions we will study in this series, the lineage of their teachings plays an important role. This is a necessary consideration when looking for qualified and respected teachers in any area of study we wish to pursue because it establishes the basis, beliefs, context, and intent of the information. Each of the eight areas of study will be preceded by a brief lineage history.

This book presents an exploration of meditation from the Karma Kagyu lineage of Tibetan Buddhism. This is one of four major lineages of Tibetan Buddhism originating with the historical Buddha of our time, Buddha Shakyamuni. We call this a fortunate eon because the sutras say there will be 1,002 Buddhas who will come to teach. We are in a time when the teachings of Buddha Shakyamuni, the fourth Buddha of this fortunate eon, are available and still being taught and practiced around the world.

The teachings can be summarized by three aspirations to practice and uphold: (1) cultivate excellent virtue in abundance, (2) avoid wrongdoing and harmful actions, and (3) completely tame your mind. This is the teaching of the Buddha. These may be simple to say but can be hard to follow! There are many ways to practice these three profound aspirations. All spiritual traditions profess to teach behaviors that lead to a happy and fulfilled life, but few give such precise methods for doing so.

The proof of the wisdom of the teaching always lies in the direct experience of its application in our lives. We are advised to put these teachings to the test: listen, contemplate, and practice these instructions. Just as when you go to see the doctor for a problem you are having, with these teachings, you will get the diagnosis, the prognosis, and the treatment to cure the ailment. However, it is not enough to just get the diagnosis and the prescription for the medicine to cure our *dis-ease*; we must then take the medicine and follow the doctor's instructions until we get the desired result. Consider being like a good patient wishing to escape pain and suffering, and follow the advice being offered to you by this Supreme Physician and spiritual friend.

This perspective is a multifaceted approach to finding the truth through a transformative process of change that is an opportunity for each of us to awaken to the true potential of who we are and what we can become.

Before we go further, I wish to clarify the title of our book and why I chose it. Having an intellectual understanding of the meaning of the words and having the direct experience of wisdom, compassion, and awakening are very different things. This book is about methods and practices that will lead to the realization of those words, the essence of the Buddha's teaching. These gifts are offered to you, and I wholeheartedly wish they are of benefit to you. May you enjoy the reading or listening as much as I enjoyed the writing.

Wisdom

Wisdom is considered one of the most important qualities to cultivate on the spiritual path. Wisdom is seen as the key to understanding the nature of reality and the path leading to liberation from suffering. There are two types of wisdom: mundane wisdom and supermundane wisdom.

Mundane wisdom refers to the knowledge gained through our conventional schooling associated with our relative experiences of the world through our five senses.

Supermundane wisdom, on the other hand, is the wisdom that arises from direct insight into the nature of reality. This type of wisdom is developed through the practice of meditation and the cultivation of mindfulness. It involves seeing things as they really are, without the distortion of attachment, aversion, and ignorance.

It is wisdom that leads one to overcome ignorance and the causes of suffering. By developing wisdom, one can see the true nature of reality and understand the interdependent nature of all things. This leads to the development of compassion and the desire to help others alleviate their suffering.

Wisdom is realized through the cultivation of mindfulness, meditation, and insight. By practicing mindfulness, one can develop the ability to stay aware and grounded in the present moment. Through meditation, one can develop the ability to focus the mind and develop mental clarity. And by cultivating insight, we develop the ability to see things as they really are and overcome mental and emotional hindrances through the meditative absorption called *samadhi*.

The role of wisdom in Buddhism is to develop a deep understanding of who we truly are and recognize the path to liberation from suffering. With wisdom, one develops the qualities of compassion, kindness, and equanimity. This ultimately leads to the direct realization of our Buddha-nature.

Compassion

Compassion is another central concept in Buddhism and is considered another necessary quality to cultivate on the spiritual path. It is the heartfelt wish for beings to be free from suffering and the causes of suffering. Compassion is closely related to the concept of *bodhichitta*, which is the mind that aspires to attain enlightenment for the benefit of all beings. Compassion is considered important for several reasons.

- ***It helps alleviate suffering.*** Compassion is the antidote to suffering. By cultivating compassion, one can develop a deep understanding of the nature of suffering and a strong desire to help others alleviate their pain and dissatisfaction.
- ***It leads to the development of wisdom.*** Compassion is also closely related to the development of wisdom. By cultivating compassion and developing a deep understanding of the nature of suffering, one develops the ability to see things clearly without the overlay of our hopes and fears. We say wisdom and compassion are like the two wings of a bird; both are needed to take us to our destination.
- ***It helps strengthen relationships.*** Compassion also plays an important role in strengthening relationships. By cultivating compassion, one can develop empathy and understanding for others, which can help create more harmonious relationships. There are practices specifically designed to cultivate compassion, such as the practice of *Tonglen*, which we will also study. This involves the practice of a special meditation to take away the suffering of others and give them happiness, health, and peace of mind. By practicing these techniques, one develops a deep sense of compassion and further nurtures the qualities of wisdom, kindness, and inner peace.

Awakened Mind

An *Awakened Mind* refers to the mind that has realized its true nature and is free from the distortions of attachment, aversion, and ignorance. This mind is often referred to as Buddha-nature, the potential for enlightenment that exists within all beings.

The Awakened Mind is the mind of a Buddha, a fully awakened being who has achieved complete liberation from suffering and attained perfect wisdom and compassion. All beings have the potential to awaken to this true nature and achieve enlightenment. This Awakened Mind has vast and innumerable qualities, such as:

- **Wisdom:** the Awakened Mind is characterized by perfect wisdom, which is the ability to see things as they are and to know the nature of reality.
- **Compassion:** the Awakened Mind also is characterized by perfect compassion, which is the heartfelt wish for beings to be free from suffering and the causes of suffering.
- **Equanimity:** the Awakened Mind is characterized by a sense of equanimity, which is the ability to remain balanced and calm in the face of all circumstances. It is also the ability to treat all beings equally, without bias or prejudice.
- **Non-Dual Awareness:** the Awakened Mind is characterized by a sense of non-dual awareness, which is the ability to see the interconnectedness of all things and the absence of a fixed, independent self.

The cultivation of the Awakened Mind is the central goal of practice. Through the practice of meditation and mindfulness, one can begin to develop an understanding of the nature of the mind and develop the qualities of wisdom, compassion, and equanimity. However, the qualities of the enlightened mind go far beyond the limitation of cognitive understanding. Fortunately, we can gradually overcome mental misconceptions and emotional distortions and experience the all-encompassing nature of the mind.

We are what we think. All that we are arises from our thoughts. With our thoughts, we make the world.

–Buddha Shakyamuni

One

Life and Teachings of the Buddha

ॐ ॐ ॐ ────────────────────────

I n this chapter, we will present an introduction to the life of the Buddha and an overview of his teachings.

Figure 1: Shakyamuni Buddha

The Buddha: A Brief History of His Enlightenment

There are many wonderful and scholarly books written on the life of the Buddha. I recommend reading such books to more deeply acquaint yourself with this most remarkable man.

The Buddha was born about 2,600 years ago, around 560 BCE, on a full-moon day in May. His mother, Queen Mahamaya, had a dream of a beautiful six-tusked white elephant entering her womb. She felt great peace and joy when she awakened from her dream. She soon realized her condition of being with child and shared this with her husband, King Suddhodana, who was delighted with the news. It had been the king's fervent wish to have an heir to the throne.

Some months later, the queen traveled from the palace in Kapilavastu to Devadaha, her parental home, to give birth, which was the custom of the time. But that was not to be! Halfway between the two cities in the beautiful Lumbini Grove under the shade of flowering sala trees and while holding the branch of a sala tree in full blossom, it is said she effortlessly and painlessly gave birth to her son, who emerged from her side. Many accounts say he then took seven steps in all four cardinal directions and announced his intention to free all beings from suffering.

He was now the prince of the small kingdom of Kapilavastu. On the fifth day following the birth, his father gathered a group of sages to help him choose an appropriate name for the new prince. The astrologers, priests, and sages agreed on the name Siddhartha, which means "one whose purpose is achieved." They also predicted he would become a powerful ruler and universal monarch, or he would renounce the world, become a Buddha, and deliver humanity from ignorance and suffering.

After watching the prince, the sage named Kala Devala (also called Asita) who was renowned for his wisdom and clairvoyant powers, smiled and told the king the prince would one day go in search of the truth and become an enlightened Buddha. He then began to cry. This was very disturbing to the king. The concerned king asked, "Why did you smile and are now crying?"

Kala Devala replied, "The smile for having the privilege to see this being who is destined to become the enlightened Buddha. And crying because I will not live long enough to receive his teachings. Rejoice, for your son will become the greatest being in the world."

These predictions concerned the king and would very much influence his behavior toward his son.

On the seventh day after Queen Mahamaya gave birth to Siddhartha, she passed away. Young Siddhartha was then cared for by his mother's sister, Prajapati. He had the best education and became skilled in many branches of knowledge and the arts and easily excelled at everything.

It was his father's ardent wish that his son would marry, bring up a family, and be his successor to the throne. However, he often recalled the prediction of the sage Kala Devala and feared that the prince would one day give up his royal heritage to lead the life of an ascetic yogi. Lacking nothing of the earthly joys of this life, Siddhartha lived surrounded by every luxury and pleasure. King Suddhodana did everything he could to protect Siddhartha from the miseries of the world, but that only heightened the prince's curiosity.

Siddhartha went to school with the other children of noble families, but it was quickly noticed how proficient he was in learning a wide range of topics, including languages and mathematics and went beyond what his teachers could provide. He was also skilled in sports and arts such as wrestling, archery and military arts. He came from the warrior class.

There is one event in his young life that seemed to make a big impression on him and was the catalyst for his pursuing a life of meditation. At the age of seven, young Siddhartha went to an annual ploughing festival with his father, King Suddhodana. At the festival, Siddhartha was taken to a large Rose-apple tree and placed on a special royal couch. While seated on the couch, he fell into deep meditative absorption. His attendants returned later and found him in a profound state of samadhi. In addition, the shadow of the tree under which he was meditating had not moved as the sun traversed the sky protecting the young prince from the sun. This is said to be the first of his meditative experiences and had a profound and lasting effect on him.

When Siddhartha was sixteen, his father decided it was time for his son to marry. The king threw a lavish party and invited all the eligible young women in the kingdom to come and present themselves to the young prince. Siddhartha's choice was Yasodhara, also sixteen, a young and beautiful woman of the Shakya clan. The king was very happy, and they were married in regal style in the palace.

Later, as a young man, there were four outings that the prince took with his charioteer, Channa. Through a succession of experiences, he was impressed by things he had not seen before: He saw a crippled man weakened by old age. He saw the sickness of a passerby, frail and weak from disease. He saw a procession of mournful family members and friends carrying the corpse of a loved one for cremation. He saw death and realized it was an inevitable consequence of birth. He recognized that even he, his beloved wife, and all his family and friends, without exception, would experience the suffering of aging, sickness, and death.

Soon after this revelation, he saw a monk calmly and peacefully walking with downcast eyes. He was moved by the serene and tranquil countenance of the man. He learned from Channa that the monk had renounced the world to live a life seeking the truth. These events greatly affected him, and he returned home in deep reflection. At twenty-nine years of age, Siddhartha left his wife, his newborn son Rahula, his royal heritage, and the palace of his birth. He renounced the world to become an ascetic wanderer.

After six years of wandering and studying with many acclaimed teachers, he quickly surpassed their level. He also found his extreme asceticism was not helpful. He realized his body needed nourishment to maintain the strength necessary for continuing on the path. He parted ways with the five yogis he had been traveling with and went on alone.

One day Siddhartha was exhausted and near death but still fiercely determined to achieve his goal of enlightenment. Siddhartha stopped and gratefully took shelter and rested beneath a large Banyan tree by the Neranjara River.

There is an interesting story about this time in the Buddha's life that I would like to add here. It is mentioned in the sutras that in a nearby village called Senani, there lived a young, rich, and beautiful girl named Sujata, who prayed for a suitable husband and a healthy son. She waited many years but was not successful. People told her to go to a certain Banyan tree near the Neranjara River and pray to the tree god to give her a husband and a son. She did as the people advised, and soon after, she got married and had a handsome and healthy son.

Sujata was extremely happy and wished to show her appreciation to that tree god for giving her all she had asked for. She fed her cows a special food so the cow's milk would be exceptionally rich and sweet. She wanted to get the sweetest and most nourishing milk for the tree god. As she was preparing her offering, she saw her attendant coming back from cleaning and getting the area ready at the foot of the tree, where her offering was to take place.

Very happy and excited, her attendant told Lady Sujata she had seen the tree god meditating at the foot of the tree. Sujata was delighted and took even more care with preparing the milk rice and poured it into a golden bowl. Taking the delicious milk rice, they went to the tree. Sujata saw what appeared to her to be the tree god sitting serenely in meditation; she did not know that this was Siddhartha. She bowed with respect and offered her gift of milk rice. She prayed that he would be successful in accomplishing his wishes, just as she had been successful in accomplishing hers.

Siddhartha ate the nourishing, sweet, thick milk rice. He felt rejuvenated and strengthened and took a ceremonial and refreshing bath in the Neranjara River. When he came out of the river, he took the golden bowl that had contained the offering and threw it in the river. He stated, "If I am to succeed in becoming a Buddha today, let this bowl go upstream, but if not, let it go downstream."

The golden bowl floated upstream in the middle of the river! We owe Sujata a debt of gratitude for her assistance to the Buddha at this critical juncture. There still is a small shrine on the banks of the Neranjara dedicated to Sujata and her good deed.

With renewed strength, that evening Siddhartha made his way to the Bodhi tree (*Ficus Religiosa*), also known as the "Tree of Enlightenment." This is where all Buddhas of this fortunate eon will attain perfect Buddhahood. He met the grass cutter, Sotthiya, on the way who gave him a large bundle of Kusha grass used by Brahmins to sit on. The grass is considered sacred and Siddhartha placed the grass under the Bodhi tree as his seat. Facing east, he sat in the meditation posture under that riverside Bodhi tree in Bodhgaya, India. He continued sitting in deep meditative absorption, determined to sit until he found the truth or died trying.

He then was attacked and wooed by the demon king, Mara, with many visions to distract him, yet he remained steady in his meditative state. As he continued in ever-deepening contemplation throughout the full-moon night, he experienced with clarity the nature of his mind. He never broke his resolve and gained direct insights in three stages that arose during the three watches of the night.

In the first watch of the night, after settling and stabilizing his mind, the Buddha contemplated and understood the pattern of the arising of suffering in his life. In the second watch of the night, the Buddha saw and understood the arising of suffering in all other beings in the six realms of existence and realized the causes of their suffering. In the third watch of the night and with great insight, he penetrated the nature of the causal pattern of existence itself, calling it *pratityasamutpada* or dependent origination.

These habitual patterns of causes and conditions create karma, the complex web of actions and results responsible for our suffering. He had awakened to the most supreme wisdom and understood things as they truly are. At the age of thirty-five on the full moon in the month of Vesak, he became the Fully Enlightened Buddha, "the Awakened One."

The Buddha, also known as the 'Supreme Physician', analyzed our condition like a physician diagnosing the sickness of his patient. He first diagnosed the illness. He next stated the cause for the arising of the illness and proclaimed there was a remedy for its removal. Last, he prescribed the remedy to cure the illness. Suffering is our illness, and craving and attachment are the root cause of this illness. Removing our attachment and craving is the remedy, as it removes the suffering. The medicine for doing so is the Noble Eightfold Path. We will now explore his teachings in greater detail.

The Buddha's First Teachings

Forty-nine days after his enlightenment, the Buddha wished to begin teaching. This was not to establish a new religion but to liberate all beings from their suffering. He journeyed to Deer Park in Sarnath near Varanasi in Northern India. Through his clairvoyance, he knew he would find the five seekers with whom he had previously traveled. When he arrived, they didn't immediately accept him because he had left them to go his own way. It was here that he began teaching.

The Buddha started by sharing the first of three teachings, where he showed the stages of the path leading to the full awakening of the Buddha. They are known as the three turnings of the Wheel of Dharma. This also describes the different aspects of training known as *the three Yanas. Yana* is Sanskrit for a vehicle that can transport us across the river from samsara (suffering) to the other shore (nirvana). (*Our Dharma center is called Gainesville Karma Thegsum Choling and means a place where the three Yanas are taught.*)

The Buddha's instruction on the first *Yana* began with the Four Noble Truths, which is the foundation of his teaching. He also taught

Abhidharma (Buddhist psychology), the selflessness of the individual, Vinaya (proper conduct), karma, and aspects of establishing a meditative mind, *Shamatha* and *Vipashyana*. These teachings on meditation and other topics would come to be known by various names, such as the Foundation Vehicle, Hinayana (Small Vehicle), Shravakayana (Vehicle of Hearers) who have heard the teaching but are not practitioners, and Pratyekabuddhayana (Solitary Realizer) whose attainment is superior to the Shravakas because of their greater accumulation of merit and wisdom. However, this is not the complete realization of a fully enlightened Buddha. These categories are not so much determined by doctrines, schools or belief systems, as they are by the internal motivation and intention of the practitioner.

In the Hinayana path, the emphasis is on personal liberation with the intention to escape the samsaric world of suffering and attain the bliss of nirvana. Hinayana is sometimes inaccurately referred to as Theravada (The Doctrine of the Elders). Hinayana does not include the Theravada traditions of Buddhism as currently practiced in countries such as, Sri Lanka, Myanmar, Thailand, and Cambodia.

Samsara is cyclic existence arising from a being's grasping and persistent attachment to a perceived self. This is further characterized as rebirth in one of six possible realms of existence in which a particular kind of suffering is experienced. This can be understood as a type of physical and/or psychological state brought about by a lack of understanding and resulting in suffering, anxiety, and dissatisfaction. It is through following the Noble Eightfold Path that liberation from samsara is achieved.

When those five seekers heard this first turning of the Wheel of Dharma, they understood and became his students. They traveled together as the Buddha continued to teach the Dharma. He kindly taught a progression of teachings according to the student's needs, capabilities, and levels of understanding.

The second turning of the Wheel of Dharma represents the Mahayana (Greater Vehicle) view of the Bodhisattvas; it is also called *Bodhisattvayana*.

The emphasis was on emptiness, as presented in the Prajnaparamita sutras on Buddha-nature and compassion. According to this teaching, enlightenment is available to all beings: it is our Buddha-nature. Another significant aspect of the Buddha's teaching is the path of the Bodhisattva. A Bodhisattva is a being who is destined to be a Buddha but has vowed not to enter into nirvana until all beings attain enlightenment.

The third turning of the Wheel is the second half of the Mahayana teachings that took place in several locations, beginning in Vaishali. It is also called Vajrayana, Tantrayana, and Mantrayana. In this teaching, the Buddha expands the teachings of the second turning by further describing emptiness and presenting the view of *Tatagatagarbha* or Buddha-nature. He explains the luminous nature of emptiness and the potential for Buddhahood present and unchanging within each of us.

For forty-five years following his awakening, Buddha Shakyamuni taught with great skill and compassion in a way that would clearly point out the path to liberation and true freedom for millions of followers.

It should also be noted that there was a fundamental difference in the teachings of the Buddha and the religion of the Brahmins in India at that time. This was concerning the caste system based on occupation. There were four groups delineated in the caste system: (1) the Brahmins were the highest class, consisting of priests, scholars and teachers; (2) the Kshatriyas were the warrior and ruling class who held positions of power, such as kings and ministers, and to which Siddhartha's family belonged; (3) the Vaishyas were the class of merchants, traders, and farmers; and (4) the Shudras were the menial workers and servants to the other three classes. Below these, there was a caste outside of these four, and its people were considered outcastes, the untouchables, the lowest of the low. Although social movements and reforms have transformed the caste system in India, there are still remnants. Even today, some still consider themselves polluted if the shadow of an untouchable should touch them!

But the Buddha taught that everyone had Buddha-nature and could realize the truth. He taught the Dharma to anyone who wished to awaken to that truth. These were revolutionary ideas for that time, and the teachings of the Buddha were considered dangerous and subversive by the Brahmins.

He left this earthly existence, achieving *parinirvana*, at age eighty in the town of Kushinagar in Northern India, near the border with Nepal. *Parinirvana* is when someone has attained nirvana during their lifetime and after death is released from samsara, karma, and rebirth.

There is some controversy about the Buddha's death. We know he died from food poisoning after accepting a meal from Chunda, the blacksmith. The texts differ on the specifics of the meal. He was offered what was called *sukara maddava* (pig's delight). Some say it was boiled pork, and others say that is the name of a truffle, a type of mushroom. Upon seeing the *sukara maddava* food, the Buddha asked Chunda to only serve it to him and then bury the remainder. According to the *Mahaparinirvana* sutra, the Buddha announced he would soon attain *parinirvana* and abandon his earthly body. This would be his last meal. Buddha's final words to the attendant monks and lay followers were, "All composite things are perishable. Strive for your own liberation with diligence."

Although the Buddha Shakyamuni's physical form has left this world, his kindness and compassion for all sentient beings persists. There were many Buddhas before him, and there will be many Buddhas in the future. All beings have this innate wisdom called Buddha-nature; it is who we truly are. It is because of our Buddha-nature that we can and will become Buddhas. It is our destiny. The only difference between us and the Buddha Shakyamuni is that we have not yet awakened to our true nature. It is obscured like the sun behind the clouds but always is there. It is immaculate and stainless, and there is nothing we can do to tarnish or improve it. Awakening to our Buddha-nature is waking from our dreamlike state into the clear awareness of our natural mind. This is who we truly are!

Two

The Three Yanas:
Turning the Wheel of Dharma

$\mathcal{B}$ $\mathcal{B}$ $\mathcal{B}$ ————————————————————————

We will now explore the Buddha's teaching in more detail. These teachings on the three turnings of the Wheel of Dharma contain the teachings of the Hinayana, the Mahayana, and the Vajrayana. It is an important part of our journey to study these three main vehicles, or methods of practice, taught by the Buddha.

The First Turning of the Wheel of Dharma: The Four Noble Truths

In his first teaching, the Buddha taught the Four Noble Truths and explained relative and ultimate reality. These teachings are commonly referred to as Hinayana. *Hinayana* means "Small Vehicle." This is not meant to be pejorative but has to do with one's motivation.

The first teaching of the Buddha after his enlightenment was to the five yogis he traveled with prior to continuing on his own. This is the teaching of the Four Noble Truths: (1) truth of suffering, (2) truth of the origin of suffering, (3) truth of the cessation of suffering, and (4) truth of the path that leads to the cessation of suffering.

He presented these four truths in two sets of two. If we examine these Four Noble Truths, we will find that the first Noble Truth, suffering, is the result caused by the second Noble Truth, the origin of suffering. The third Noble Truth, the cessation of suffering, is seen as the result of the fourth Noble Truth, the path that leads to the cessation of suffering. Simply put, we see the Four Noble Truths are causes and results. The first two truths are the causes that result in suffering and the second two truths are the causes that result in nirvana, enlightenment, and freedom from suffering. Let's explore this a little further.

The Truth of Suffering

The first Noble Truth makes it clear that there is suffering. It is not just a question of eliminating the suffering itself, but we must also eliminate the causes of suffering. Once we remove the causes of suffering, then automatically, suffering is no longer present. To eliminate this suffering, we must become aware of the second Noble Truth, the truth of interdependent origination—*tendrel*. This teaching contained in the Four Noble Truths is how the Middle Way view is to be cultivated and practiced.

The Buddha said we must "know" suffering. What does that mean? Because everything that exists or that can be experienced on the relative level of reality is made of composite elements, causes, and conditions and is impermanent, its composition will eventually break down. The first step is to bring this realization onto the path of our awakening mind to recognize and acknowledge it. He outlined this as a doctor diagnosing an illness. For most of us, it is natural to immediately think suffering is to be avoided, prevented, or ignored. But this is not what the Buddha taught. He said suffering is to be *known*. While there are many subcategories, we will consider three basic patterns of suffering in our lives:

1. ***The suffering of suffering.*** This is the one we are all familiar with. The Buddha called it the suffering of the pain of birth, old age, sickness, and death. This takes many forms in our lives. Disease, broken bones, accidents, stubbing your toe, and the myriad possibilities that upset us daily.

2. ***The suffering of change.*** It can be the rags-to-riches story but also the unknown circumstances that change the narrative from riches to rags. For example, we usually think it would be good to win the lottery. However, there are more stories about how winning changed individual lives in a very painful way. Or the simple twist of fate that changes from our getting the dream job to getting fired. Inevitably, changes occur in our lives. We are creatures of habit, and for most of us, our resistance to change is a type of suffering we experience on a regular basis.

3. ***All-pervasive change.*** This is often overlooked as suffering, but it is a general feeling of malaise, an existential dilemma, and anxiety and insecurity we all feel. Even when we are happy, we still feel doubtful, uneasy, and dissatisfied, knowing it will not last. This is *samsara* and what the Buddha meant when he said we must know suffering and consequently will come to understand its cause. But what is its cause?

Truth of the Cause of Suffering

The second Noble Truth is the diagnosis of the cause or the origin of our suffering. Once we realize that suffering, *dis-ease*, or dissatisfaction exists, we next discover where it comes from. It is taught that our suffering originates in our false belief in a truly existent, permanent self. From this fixation arises what are called the three poisons of attachment, aggression, and delusion. From these "poisons" come further negative emotions and all aspects of suffering. When we begin to look deeper into our behavior in body, speech, and mind, we realize the main source of suffering that afflicts us is our mind and attitude.

If we want to overcome our experience of suffering, we will have to investigate and learn how to uproot our endless forms of excessive desire, craving, grasping, clinging, and attachment. And why should we uproot these tendencies? It is by uprooting these habitual patterns that we end suffering. We see how suffering is connected to our actions. This is why to eliminate suffering we must become aware of the second Noble Truth of interdependent origination, also known as dependent origination.

When we speak about an action, we are also speaking about the karmic consequences of the action. We are constantly accumulating three different categories or types of karma, depending on motivation and intention of our action: negative, positive, or neutral. All the thoughts and actions we engage in will inevitably leave their karmic residue in our mind that is either positive, negative, or neutral, depending on our motivations and intentions.

For example, a thought such as hatred, which has tremendous energy and strength behind it, will leave its karmic seed in the mind stream, which will manifest as anger and hatred when the causes and conditions arise. This is as certain as when you plant an acorn, it will result in an oak tree. When we talk about interdependent origination, we are talking about the root cause of suffering, which is karma and disturbing emotions (*klesha*).

Karma is a Sanskrit word that means "activity," and *klesha*, in Sanskrit, means "mental defilement" or "mental poison." Those unfamiliar with the Buddha's teaching might attribute happiness and suffering to some external cause. They may think happiness and suffering come from something outside of our control. However, what we experience is not dependent on external factors but on our self-arisen previous karma. With this understanding, we can skillfully begin to remove the causes of suffering.

The Truth of the Cessation of Suffering

The third Noble Truth is the goal and why the Buddha came to teach. He said he was here to show us the way to end our suffering and free ourselves. If the Buddha stopped with the first two truths, that would be very unfortunate indeed! We first looked at how given our human condition, suffering and dissatisfaction are ubiquitous in our lives. Then we looked at the cause of the suffering arising from the three poisons, karmic causes and conditions, and our false belief in a truly existent, permanent self.

In the third Noble Truth, the truth of the cessation of suffering, Buddha taught that there is a remedy for the suffering that pervades our samsaric existence. Samsara means, because of our misunderstanding of the nature of reality, that we continually go round and round, life after life. Our experience of old age, sickness, death, and rebirth is the result of the accumulated karma experienced in previous lives until now. We will continue to reincarnate, life after life, until our karmic seeds are finally exhausted, and Buddhahood is achieved.

The good news is that we *do* have control over our suffering. We are the only ones responsible for the karma and disturbing emotions we ourselves create. We don't need to look to anyone else to remove our suffering.

As we have seen with the truth of interdependent origination, what we experience is entirely in our hands. Simply put, virtuous actions result in happiness, and unvirtuous actions result in suffering. Fortunately, our suffering is only temporary, and we can go beyond it while still living in this world. It *is* possible to achieve real peace of mind in this life! Attaining this peace of mind means freedom from desire and attachment. One's mind will no longer be afflicted by mental delusions and emotional afflictions, and we can rest in the mind's clear awareness. We can be at peace, in tranquility, and at ease. When we have discovered the origin of suffering and have uprooted its causes, our ego-clinging and disturbing emotions will cease. In this state, all mental delusions and emotional afflictions have been overcome, and the mind is liberated from habitual fixations.

The Truth of the Path Leading to the Cessation of Suffering

The fourth Noble Truth is called "the Truth of the Path" because it leads to the ultimate goal. We follow the path step by step and stage by stage until we have completed our journey. This is the cure that leads to the cessation of suffering. When the Buddha taught these Four Noble Truths, he showed the cause-and-effect relationship. He showed how neither our suffering nor our liberation are random occurrences. There is a cause for our suffering and, equally, a cause for ending our suffering and achieving liberation.

What is the means that was taught to achieve the goal of liberation? The method for progressing along the path to enlightenment is known as the "Noble Eightfold Path." It consists of training in three areas: morality, meditation, and wisdom.

Morality means cultivating virtue through discipline to protect oneself from wrongdoing and accumulating the negative karma that leads to suffering. It includes Right Speech, Right Action, Right Livelihood, and Right Effort. The training in meditation or *samadhi* is through the cultivation of tranquility meditation, *Shamatha*, and penetrating insight, *Vipashyana*. It includes Right Mindfulness and Right Concentration.

This Noble Eightfold Path describes the following trainings in *Right View, Right Thought, Right Speech, Right Action, Right Livelihood, Right Effort, Right Mindfulness, and Right Concentration.* These provide methods for working with and overcoming our ego-clinging and disturbing emotions. This is called the path of individual liberation, known as Hinayana, the path of the *arhats*, and is followed by all schools of Buddhism. If we are to follow this Noble Eightfold Path, it is essential that we know what this path is and how to practice it correctly. Briefly, these eight are as follows:

1. ***Right View*** is the guide to the entire path. It is the foundation for the study of the path to liberation from suffering and for each petal of the Golden Eight-Petaled Lotus. Our study must begin with the proper motivation. It is important that we have an experiential understanding and not just an intellectual or theoretical knowledge. We accept responsibility for our progress step by step. In so doing, we take responsibility for our destiny. We may not be able to change circumstances in our life, but we can change our responses to them.

   Our views and beliefs are key in determining our attitudes and actions. Our views about ourselves and the world shape our perceptions and establish our values. They create the lens through which we interpret the world and the meaning of our existence. Knowing that everything arises because of causes and conditions enables us to take responsibility for our actions.

   Right View is the foundation for our spiritual journey and directs our activity in the world. As we will see, there are many levels of the Buddha's teachings. There are the *Hinayana* teachings, the *Mahayana* teachings, the *Vajrayana* teachings, and the *Mahamudra* teachings. Each of these traditions has developed its way of defining these various methods. It is important for us to continuously strive to develop the Right View in our meditation practices.

2. ***Right Thought*** expands the realization of how our thoughts and emotions are linked together. This includes the cultivation of proper motivation and scrutinizing our habitual self-centered ways of thinking to a more altruistic way of thinking. The Buddha said, "As you think, you become." Indulging in negative thoughts leads to negative actions in body, speech, and mind. On the other hand, thinking in a positive way has a positive effect on our emotions and our actions. We become more loving, caring, and compassionate to ourselves and with

others. This is based on three aspects: non-attachment, goodwill, and harmlessness. These three aspects help develop our wisdom mind and the practice of *bodhichitta*.

We can train our mind. This is enhanced by meditation. We can meditate on the suffering inherent in our constant pursuit of worldly desires and gently lead our minds toward loving-kindness and compassion. Meditation on loving-kindness is the best remedy for anger, self-cherishing, ego-clinging, and ill will.

The most effective antidote for harmlessness is meditation on compassion. In our meditation practice, we begin with developing our motivation. We are doing meditation for the benefit of all suffering beings. At the end of our meditation, we Dedicate the Merit generated from doing the practice for the happiness and well-being of everyone.

To **Dedicate the Merit** means to give this positive energy to others, with the intention of benefiting them. This can be done in various ways, for example, by mentally dedicating the merit to a person, a group of people, such as loved ones, friends, and all beings in the world—even those who might have hurt us! You can do this by simply thinking or saying, "May the merit generated by this practice be dedicated to [*say the name of the person or group*] so that they may be happy, peaceful, and free from suffering." This also can include the accumulation of merit for a specific purpose, such as the well-being of a sick person, or animal, or the success of a particular project. In this way, we offer our practice, meditation, reciting mantras, making prostrations, or performing acts of generosity, with the intention of accumulating merit for that purpose.

Furthermore, if you dedicate the virtue you accumulate to supreme awakening, you will still experience the pleasant results of that merit, abundant well-being in life after life. It will not be exhausted until the principal aim of your dedication, which is supreme awakening, has been achieved. Therefore, dedicating your merit in this way makes your virtue inexhaustible until enlightenment is reached.

3. **Right Speech** means becoming aware of speech. This step on the Noble Eightfold Path comes under morality. Our speech is very important, and we can tell a lot about a person from their speech. We can't see another person's mind, so we often judge or are judged by behavior and speech. We train in being mindful of our speech. We consider the consequences of our speech. Is it harmful or helpful?

    What are some examples we can do to develop excellent speech? One thing is reciting mantras, such as OM MANI PADME HUM, the mantra of Chenrezig, the Bodhisattva of Great Compassion. Mantra means "mind protection." Mantras such as this can be a powerful tool in transmuting negative emotions and can be used at any time and under all circumstances.

    By being mindful of Right Speech, we are developing a conscious awareness of words and what we are saying. Now more than ever, our speech can have tremendous capacity leading to either good or bad consequences. We have a wide range of arenas to express ourselves, and we interact in social media and other forms of speech, including the written word in our digital online communication. We must remain mindful of our speech.

    Right Speech has four elements. The first is abstaining from false speech or lying and cultivating truthful speech. The second is abstaining from slanderous speech and cultivating speech that promotes friendship and harmony. The third is abstaining from harsh speech, yelling, insulting, and sarcasm. The fourth is abstaining from idle chatter. This can include television, radio, magazines, and speech that is harmful and hurtful.

We often indulge in unskillful forms of speech, such as lying, gossip, harsh words, and divisive speech. This can also include how we communicate with others in what we call "body language," such as communicating negative feelings toward others with harmful gestures. This all has a direct influence on our temperament and demeanor. We try to be truthful, though this is difficult in a society that manipulates the truth and has turned falsehood and deception into a way of life that impacts us daily. It is important to be mindful of our speech.

4. ***Right Action*** is behaving consciously in ways that do not hurt others and being cognizant of the effects of our behavior on others. We do many things, and everything we do has a consequence. With Right Action, we act in ways that benefit ourselves and others. We can analyze the quality of our actions and discern between what is beneficial and what is not.

There is a story about a monk who was trying to improve his behavior. What he would do is with every skillful action in body, speech, and mind, he would put a small white pebble in his pocket, and for every unskillful action, he would put a black pebble in his pocket. At the end of the day, he would check his pockets for white and black pebbles. At first, the small black and white stones at the end of the day were relatively equal. Gradually, as he became more mindful of his behavior, at the end of the day, he only had white pebbles.

Some lay practitioners observe five precepts as their commitment to the path, but monks and nuns observe many more. The five precepts are: not killing, not taking that which is not given, not lying, not misusing intoxicants, and not engaging in sexual misconduct.

We abstain from overuse of intoxicants because it dulls the mind. We often use it as a form of escape and, over time, our habit can lead to dependence on such substances. Perhaps the most important reason to refrain from intoxicants or to keep our intake moderate is to prevent bad behavior. When under the influence of a drug or intoxicant that affects mental clarity, we are vulnerable to hurting ourselves or others, causing suffering that leads to regret and remorse.

The Buddha advised we cultivate mindfulness in all our activities. It can be as simple as doing good deeds, such as following the Golden Rule, that is "Do unto others as you would have them do unto you."

5. **Right Livelihood** is concerned with our capacity to earn a living without causing harm to ourselves or others. It has always been based on the principle of *ahimsa* or harmlessness. As we know, our livelihood means more than just our job, but also all our main daily activities and how we spend most of our time providing the necessities we need, such as having food, clothes, a roof over our head, and so on.

We spend much of our time working. Although many jobs seem harmless enough, look closely at what the company does, and avoid companies that cause harm to people, animals, or the environment. We do not wish to cause death, harm, cruelty, physical or mental pain to any living being as a consequence of how we are earning a living. Nor would we invest our resources in companies that do not promote and foster the health and happiness of others.

6. **Right Effort** is essential to accomplish anything in life. Right Effort also has the connotation of joy and enthusiasm. This is certainly what is needed on the path to total freedom from suffering and the attainment of liberation.

We make a joyful and enthusiastic effort in our meditation practice to uproot unwholesome thoughts and emotions as they arise. This will ultimately stop them from arising.

Proper effort is the energy needed to stay aware and awake in the moment to overcome our laziness. With the Right Effort, we ensure our energy is directed to wholesome states of mind.

The importance of the Right Effort is greatly stressed. Making progress on the path requires diligence, exertion, and perseverance. No one can do this for us. Our destiny is in our hands. With Right Effort, all things are possible, and we can achieve our goals.

7. *Right Mindfulness* increases our attention to our thoughts, emotions, feelings, speech, and behavior. To achieve superior meditation, we practice mindfulness, *samadhi*, the ability to rest the mind in its natural state of clear awareness. In meditation, we have mindfulness; our mind is clear, aware, and present in the moment. It is also important not to lose the thread of meditation between meditation sessions.

We learn how to carry the power of our meditation into our daily life. We become more conscious of our experiences and have the capacity to make choices as to how we wish to respond to any situation. Our response to situations does not need to be our habitual knee-jerk reactions, but a thoughtful, measured response to the current situation. We are no longer reactive; we become truly responsible for our behavior.

Mindfulness is integral to our practice of meditation and facilitates the attainment of mental stability. We train our mind to remain in the present, noting the arising of thoughts as they arise, without judgment or interpretation.

Mindfulness meditation grounds the mind firmly in the present. We are usually more like time travelers. We are frequently reflecting with nostalgia or regret about the past or projecting some fear or worry into the future, but rarely are we in the perfection of this present moment.

8. ***Right Concentration*** gives us the capacity to progress in our meditation practice. The mind becomes focused and stable. We become less distracted and more able to maintain our attention and awareness steadily for extended periods. Without the other previous steps on the Noble Eightfold Path, Right Concentration cannot arise.

   Right Concentration is developed by using two methods: tranquility meditation (*Shamatha*) and insight meditation (*Vipashyana*). They require preliminary practices, such as moral discipline, the guidance of a teacher, and a good environment conducive to meditation.

   Right Concentration develops single-pointedness of mind. This is like training a puppy. When we say "stay," the trained mind can remain focused and absorbed in meditation without distraction. That's where meditative concentration, *samadhi*, comes in. The word *samadhi* means "profound absorption." To rest in this absorption brings great benefit. It is through increasing our meditative absorption that leads to wisdom and the fruition of our practice.

   This has been a brief description of the Four Noble Truths from the Buddha's first turning of the Wheel of Dharma. All later teachings of the Buddha are based on understanding these Four Noble Truths.

The Second Turning of the Wheel of Dharma: The Two Truths

The Buddha turned the Wheel of Dharma for the second time at Vulture Peak Mountain. At that time, he taught the Perfection of Wisdom, *Prajnaparamita*, to an assembly of Bodhisattvas, monks, and a host of many other beings. He taught the complete teachings on emptiness. He said, relatively speaking, things do appear; however, they ultimately have no essential nature, no lasting and inherent existence on the level of ultimate reality.

The Two Truths: Relative and Ultimate

The teachings on relative and absolute truth are found in the second and third turnings of the Wheel of Dharma. To understand emptiness, we must distinguish between relative and absolute truth. When we gain realization into the ultimate nature of phenomenon, our everyday life the relative world does not contradict this understanding but is part of it. This is called the realization of two truths. This means that we study on the ultimate level the way things or phenomena really are, and on the conventional, relative level, we study the way things occur and appear according to the laws of interdependence.

Relative truth is our conventional reality, something on which we all agree. Relative truth includes all dualistic phenomena, including ourselves, other beings, all objects, things we see, hear, touch, and experience through our five senses. This includes all that makes up our material world. This relative world is perfect and based on the dependent origination of all phenomena. The problem is our misapprehension and misunderstanding of its nature.

Absolute truth is the reality beyond dualism, labels, and concepts. In the Mahayana, it is called emptiness, voidness, or *shunyata*. When subjected to analysis, relative phenomena disappear, and all you find is absolute truth, emptiness.

This understanding is the Perfection of Wisdom. This was taught by the Buddha in the Prajnaparamita Sutras, such as the Heart Sutra. This Sutra is recited and chanted by monks and lay Buddhists around the world. It is from this Sutra that we find the often quoted saying, "Form is emptiness; emptiness is also form. Emptiness is no other than form; form is no other than emptiness." It is this realization that leads to liberation and Buddhahood.

From the Mahayana perspective, the Buddha's second turning of the Wheel of Dharma is seen as the ultimate and definitive teaching. The Buddha taught that all conditioned existence is identified by the "three marks of existence:" impermanence (*anicca*), suffering or dissatisfaction (*dukkha*), and no-self or egolessness (*anatta*). These "three marks" apply to all conditioned things. This is accepted in the Hinayana and Mahayana schools.

We touched on this when discussing the three kinds of suffering but need to further clarify the term *anatta* or "selflessness or egolessness." This can be a little more difficult to grasp. The Buddha taught there is no unchanging, permanently existing self that inhabits our bodies. We do not have a fixed absolute identity. The experience of "I" continuing through life as a separate, singular being is an illusion. What we call the self is a construct of physical, mental, and sensory processes that are independent and constantly in flux.

It is the illusion of a separate, permanent self that chains us to our suffering and dissatisfaction. We put most of our energy into protecting this image of a self, trying to gratify it and clinging to impermanent things we think will enhance it. The belief in this separate, permanent self leads to the craving that, according to the Four Noble Truths, is the source of our suffering.

This teaching, especially the practice of the Noble Eightfold Path, provides the medicine to remove our misunderstandings so we become less self-centered and less attached to impermanent things. As we investigate and meditate upon the truth of these three marks of existence, we will develop the "factors of enlightenment," such as equanimity. In so doing, we will develop stability and serenity.

In addition to the teachings on emptiness, there is one more thing the Buddha taught in this cycle of teachings that also is important and that I always emphasize. He taught the importance of cultivating *bodhichitta*, usually translated as "mind of enlightenment" or "awakened heart." This is the heartfelt wish that all beings, not just oneself, may attain the state of perfect enlightenment. The Bodhisattvas pledge themselves by taking a vow to commit to work diligently to lead all beings to that enlightened state. This commitment to working for the welfare of suffering beings until enlightenment is reached is the hallmark of the Mahayana path. When we realize selflessness and combine this with loving-kindness and compassion, it becomes the perfect Mahayana expression of *bodhichitta*.

The Third Turning of the Wheel of Dharma: Buddha-Nature

In the third turning of the Wheel of Dharma to his retinue of Bodhisattvas, monks, and a host of other beings, the Buddha went further into the nature of mind. This teaching differs from the Sutric approach of the Hinayana and Mahayana, which is more gradual and takes many lifetimes, while the Vajrayana approach is considered faster, more direct, and experiential. Both approaches seek to achieve the same realization; however, they do so by different means.

This third teaching is referred to by various names, such as Vajrayana, Tantrayana, and Mantrayana. It includes the visualization of peaceful and wrathful deities, *yidams*, in pure realms and recitation of sacred sounds called mantras. The mind's nature is not mere nothingness, a state of nonexistence, but luminous awareness beyond conceptual fabrication. It is the direct experience of the mind's emptiness and lucid clarity, endowed with immeasurable qualities.

The Buddha clarified the nature of mind by introducing *Tathagatagarbha*, also called Buddha-nature, which is the seed for our realization of Buddhahood. The Buddha described this as our fundamental nature that has been primordially and utterly pure from the beginning. It has never changed from beginningless time. This essence is inconceivably profound, vast, and deathless. However, it is taught that this potential seed of enlightenment, our Buddha-nature, is hidden by temporary obscurations, in the same way the sun may be temporarily obscured and concealed by the clouds in the sky. This prevents us from directly apprehending it. By practicing in the above-mentioned ways, we can remove the obscurations and directly apprehend the brilliant nature of our mind.

This completes a brief review of the Buddha's teaching on the three *Yanas* and the three turnings of the Wheel of Dharma. These trainings and methods play a vital role in the fundamental teaching of the Buddha: cultivate virtue, avoid wrongdoing, and tame your mind. This is the teaching of the Buddha. The Buddha only taught one Dharma that people heard in different ways, depending on their aptitude. These teachings have been repeated for hundreds of years. There have been different understandings, and consequently, different schools have developed over 2,600 years. The Hinayana is the foundation for the Mahayana; the Mahayana and Hinayana supports the Vajrayana and is indispensable to it.

Dharma Is the Map to Reach the Destination

It is essential that we begin with Right View. Without this "Right View," we can become confused. These teachings are called the Dharma and serve as the map, and our teachers serve as kind guides on our journey. We need a guide who can show us the path clearly to prevent us from taking wrong turns and dead ends. We are so fortunate to have these teachings available to us and have teachers who can guide us on the path to Buddhahood!

Without discovering and following the correct path, we will not meet the conditions necessary for success. By following this path, we can realize the nature of our mind. But to free ourselves from samsara, we must take the first step on that path and continue with joyful perseverance to the completion of our journey. There are two faults that can affect progress on the path to freedom: first, not starting on the path; and second, not continuing to the end.

Buddhas and Bodhisattvas of the past began their journey the same as we do. They entered the path as ordinary beings just like us. It was only through proper guidance of their teachers that they immersed themselves and integrated the teaching into their daily lives and achieved enlightenment. The difference between enlightened beings and ordinary beings is not what is seen, but in the *way* they are seen. From the perspective of the enlightened mind, everything is an expression of our Buddha-nature, and it is insubstantial and empty of any inherent existence. This experience of direct seeing into the nature of reality is the essence of enlightenment. It is also the basis for the cultivation of *bodhichitta*, the motivation to benefit all sentient beings.

One who has awakened to their true nature sees that those who have not recognized this truth will cling and hold fast to dualistic concepts with fixed ideas. This misapprehension and wrong view will lead to further suffering for them. The Bodhisattva, through the force of their strong motivation, seeks the happiness of all suffering beings by removing the source of their self-imposed suffering, ego-clinging. The *bodhichitta* generated by Bodhisattvas is directed equally to all beings. The main point is that someone who understands this acts with naturally arising compassion for all beings wandering in samsara.

Training in the Preliminaries

You have now been introduced to some important concepts of Buddhist thought. We will now consider ways we can easily put it into practice. More and more people are investigating the ideas related to these teachings, such as mindfulness, inner peace, meditation, loving-kindness, and compassion.

There have even been recent discoveries in science that give us new insights into the mind. Researchers are finding many correlations in the teachings of the Buddha that are now coming to light in the scientific community. These contemporary topics were considered and taught by the Buddha. He taught a path to enlightenment. It doesn't matter what your background is, whether you're an atheist, agnostic, Christian, or a follower of any other system of belief.

The teachings of the Buddha can lead to a happier, richer life. His words are not concerned with dogma or academics. They invite us to approach reality as it is and to deepen our experience of being alive. We see the same universal sentiments echoed by many religions. We are finding these teachings are still relevant. In fact, we see many of these teachings resurfacing today among the psychologists and contemporary self-help methodologies based on this realization. The Buddha cautioned us not to take his teachings on pure belief, but to put them to the test in our life, to practice them and see if it is true for each of us.

Although Buddhism is viewed as a religion and has many millions of followers, it isn't about worshipping a divine being. It is about awakening to the truth of who we are and experiencing it directly.

The question now becomes how we cultivate the motivation and courage to practice this path the Buddha taught. We must start with the recognition of our good fortune of being born human and encountering these Dharma teachings so essential to our progress on the path to awakening. We have been wandering in samsara for a very long time. We now have a tremendous opportunity as a result of our accumulation of merit from positive actions over eons. The ripening of this good karma must not be wasted but used as a catalyst to proceed with diligence and perseverance until the goal is realized.

The preliminaries are the bases upon which we can build our practice. The contemplation of the four thoughts that turn the mind to Dharma reminds us of what is important in life. At the time of this writing, I am in my mid-seventies. From this perspective, time seems to have passed very quickly, seemingly going faster with every passing year. We must understand our situation by reflecting on these preliminary reminders so as not to waste this precious opportunity.

So how should we listen to these teachings? When we free ourselves from prejudices and cultivate an open, humble, and receptive attitude to these teachings, we become worthy vessels for the Dharma.

An example of this is found in the Zen Buddhist literature. There is a story about an egotistical scholar, who went in search of a Zen master to question and challenge him. He found a well-known teacher who was sufficiently revered, and he arrogantly requested a teaching from the master. In greeting him, the Zen master insisted on serving him a cup of tea. The master poured the tea and kept pouring the tea, even after it had spilled over the edge of the cup and onto the table and eventually onto the floor, until the man yelled out, "Stop! The cup is too full!" The master replied, "So are you."

We must be like an empty vessel: open and receptive.

Four Thoughts That Turn the Mind to Dharma

Having reviewed the Four Noble Truths, we will see how these preliminary practices, *the Four Thoughts that Turn the Mind to Dharma*, are concerned with directly seeing the Truth of Suffering and the Truth of the Cause of Suffering. With these contemplations, we train our mind away from activities that lead to suffering and toward activities that will result in freedom from suffering. These contemplations are offered as a catalyst to inspire and motivate us to pursue the Path with diligence and a sense of urgency.

The Four Thoughts to consider are:

1. How fortunate we are to have this opportunity of a precious human birth.
2. That this precious human birth is impermanent, and we should use our time wisely.
3. How we create karma through our actions and how our happiness or suffering is the result of our positive and negative actions.
4. The unsatisfactoriness of samsara and realization that the nature of samsara is suffering, resulting in the continuous cycle of rebirth in the six realms of existence.

1: Precious Human Birth

The cause for being born human is from having abandoned negative action and accumulating merit from the cultivation of positive action in the past. This precious human birth has everything we need. We come to understand how it is difficult to get and how easily it is lost. We also are fortunate to have been born at this time and must make the most of it now, when these teachings are still available to us, for this will not always be the case. These teachings will gradually decline and fade away until the future Buddha, Buddha Maitreya, comes to teach the Dharma again. However, the sutras say this will not occur for tens of thousands of years.

This gift presented to us can be seen as a precious gem. We can come to appreciate this opportunity, like being given a wish-fulfilling jewel so difficult to obtain. We can reflect on the rarity and preciousness of obtaining a human birth endowed with freedom and potential. It highlights the opportunities and favorable conditions that this human life provides for success in traveling the path to liberation.

I have respectfully paraphrased how the great eighth-century Buddhist Master Shantideva used an analogy for asking us to contemplate how difficult obtaining this precious human birth is. He advised that unless we begin to cultivate mindfulness now and put it into practice, the chances of being born human in the future is like those of a blind sea turtle poking his head through the center of a rubber inner tube (or a yoke) that's floating on a vast, churning ocean, blown by the wind in all directions. The likelihood of that blind turtle who surfaces once every hundred years poking his head up through the center of the inner tube is like our chances of being born human! We must make the most of this precious opportunity.

2: Impermanence

We find a powerful remedy for grasping at or fixating on objects through meditation on impermanence, which is the second contemplation that turns the mind to Dharma. As we contemplate the nature of impermanence, we see that all things experienced by our sense faculties are impermanent and devoid of inherent self-nature.

Contemplate the transient and impermanent nature of all phenomena. See how all things are subject to change with the passage of time. This reflection leads to the recognition of their impermanence and to the understanding that attachment to fleeting experiences and material possessions leads to suffering. We find that the degree of our suffering is the degree of our attachment. The important thing is to recognize our grasping, because as we come to understand impermanence, grasping is pacified and ultimately eliminated.

3: Karma

The third contemplation is on karma and its result. We are taught that all phenomena arise from causes and conditions, otherwise known as interdependence or dependent origination. It emphasizes that our actions have consequences, and that we are responsible for the quality of our lives. Recognizing the power of the choices we make, both positive and negative, motivates us to engage in virtuous actions and to abandon harmful ones.

Karma accumulates because of this interdependence, and it applies to everything. Thich Nhat Hanh called this *inter-being*. He would say, as he held up a sheet of paper, "See the cloud in the paper, from the cloud came the rain to nourish the seed, that created the tree, that produced the pulp that made the paper." By this analogy, he also demonstrated the law of interdependence.

4: Samsara

The Fourth Thought is the suffering of samsaric existence. We are to contemplate the unsatisfactory nature of samsara, the perpetual cycle of birth, aging, sickness, and death. This reflection is necessary to recognize the inherent suffering and dissatisfaction that is present in our worldly existence and is shown in graphic detail on the nightly news.

Within samsaric existence, there are six realms. The three lower realms include beings in the hell realms, hungry ghosts, and animals. There are also three higher realms of humans, demigods, and gods. So, when we talk about samsara, we refer to these six realms of existence.

The Buddha said that these realms are actually projections of one's mind. In the ultimate sense, the six realms of beings do not really exist. They appear as a result of the karmic predispositions of beings and manifest outwardly as the six realms of existence, just as we are experiencing this human realm based on the causes experienced in past lives. This is the fruition of karmic seeds. Understanding the unsatisfactoriness of samsara, we follow the Noble Eightfold Path, the truth that leads to the cessation of suffering and the end of samsara.

These Four Thoughts that turn the mind to Dharma are tied directly to the Four Noble Truths. These contemplations serve as a foundation for the Buddhist path and are often taught at the beginning of one's practice.

Taking Refuge

Refuge and Engendering Bodhichitta Prayer

Until I reach enlightenment, I take refuge in the
Buddha, the Dharma, and the noble Sangha.
Through the merit of accomplishing the Six Perfections, may
I achieve awakening for the benefit of all sentient beings.
(*Repeat three times.*)

In Buddhism, taking refuge is considered a fundamental step on the path to enlightenment. Taking refuge means seeking the guidance, protection, and support of the Buddha, the Dharma (his teachings), and the Sangha (the community of practitioners). It opens the door to the storehouse of the Buddha's teaching. There are many reasons why taking refuge is important; these include:

1. *Protection from suffering.* Taking refuge in the Buddha, Dharma, and Sangha is seen as a way to protect oneself from suffering. By relying on the Three Jewels, one can develop the strength and wisdom to face life's challenges and overcome them. It grants fearlessness.

2. *Guidance on the path to enlightenment.* Taking refuge also is important because it provides guidance on the path to enlightenment. By relying on the Buddha, Dharma, and Sangha,

we learn the teachings and apply them in our daily life to cultivate wisdom, compassion, and peace of mind.

3. ***The connection to a spiritual community.*** Taking refuge in the Sangha is a way to become connected to a spiritual community. Through this connection, we receive support, encouragement, and inspiration from others who are also on the path to freedom.

The Eight Benefits of Taking the Vow of Refuge:

1. When you have taken the Refuge Vow, you are a Buddhist and have formally entered the stream of Dharma, received the blessing of the Buddha, and are given full access to his teachings.
2. This vow is the basis for all other vows; without refuge, you cannot take the vows of individual liberation (lay vows), the Bodhisattva Vow, empowerments, or any other Vajrayana Vows.
3. The Vow protects you from harm.
4. It purifies your past misdeeds.
5. By doing virtuous actions, you accumulate greater merit.
6. You will not be reborn in the lower realms.
7. You have now entered the excellent path of Dharma.
8. Ultimately, you will go beyond suffering and attain Buddhahood.

We should always remember how fortunate we are to be able to take the Refuge Vow. Of all the limitless sentient beings who are wandering in samsara, so many are confused and frightened, without any source of protection or understanding. They have no reliable guide to lead them out of their physical pain and strife and the mental stress, depression, and anxiety that pervade everyday life. Fortunately, you have found such protection and can make a decision to embark on a journey that will lift you out of samsara and into the light of your Awakened Mind.

More and more people worldwide are becoming interested in meditation and are coming in contact with Buddhism. Through reading and study, they have developed the wish to take the next formal step of becoming a Buddhist. It is estimated that there are about 500 million people worldwide who call themselves Buddhist, and by definition, that means taking refuge in the Buddha, the Dharma, and the Sangha.

After you hear or read Dharma teachings and put them to the test, you are ready for the next step. It is time to consider taking refuge. It conveys much blessing. You are given a new name and a new beginning. It is also conferring a blessing with the commitments of the vow and opens the door to the community, the teachings, and the path to awakening.

The purpose of *Taking Refuge* is to serve as a guide on the path to enlightenment. Since experiencing enlightenment is our goal, the first source of refuge is the Buddha. We wish to experience perfect Buddhahood, just as he did. He showed us the path to follow to attain the goal, and if we follow the path with diligence and enthusiasm, we will attain the goal.

To achieve Buddhahood, we have to follow the path. The path is called the Dharma, and the second source of refuge is the Dharma. It is our guide, and following the unmistaken path leads to accomplishing our goal of awakening.

We also need a community with which to study and practice. The Sangha is the third refuge. Sangha members are those trained in the Dharma and who are able to guide students on the path. It is because of the devotion of the Sangha that the path taught by the Buddha was able to be passed down from teacher to student in an unbroken lineage to the present.

Practitioners begin any practice by first taking refuge and engendering *bodhichitta*.

We will now continue with our mind-training practice through the cultivation of the Four Immeasurables.

The Four Immeasurables: Cultivating Bodhichitta, the Mind of Enlightenment

The Four Immeasurables

Love

May all beings be happy and have the causes of happiness.

Compassion

May all beings be free of suffering and the causes of suffering.

Joy

May all beings never be separated from great bliss and free of suffering.

Equanimity

May all beings rest in equanimity, free of the bias of attachment
and aversion, having the same great love for all.

The meditation on the Four Immeasurables is about training our mind and the development of our human potential. We appreciate the teachings, in all traditions, that help us develop these qualities of love, compassion, joy, and equanimity. We see in our current literature and magazines that there is immense growth and interest in meditation and mindfulness. We can see this interest is growing by the increase in scientific research being published in professional journals and mainstream media.

This interest and exposure is a good sign. We're all looking for answers about how to stay healthy and balanced in this rapidly changing global environment. It is very important for the world to continue to show such interest in how to enhance positive human qualities and create sanity by encouraging contemplation and meditation.

That brings us to the Four Immeasurables, also called *Brahmaviharas* or the Four Sublime States. These are seen as the source of maintenance for our sanity. They are a set of virtues taught by the Buddha to cultivate positive emotions and attitudes towards oneself and others. The Buddha said, "Anyone unable to join one's mind with these four causes, or sources, of human sanity, will constantly be bound by the confusion of cyclic existence." He is talking about engendering the positive qualities of loving-kindness, compassion, joy, and equanimity in our daily life.

Contemplate These Four Immeasurables:

1. *Love.* The word for "loving-kindness" in Sanskrit is *maitri* or *metta* in Pali. The definition of love is wanting others to be happy; it is related to a feeling of friendship without expectation. It is a quality of mind that is unconditional, and it starts with us. It entails a heartfelt yearning for the happiness of whoever we bring to mind.

   Starting with ourselves, we wish for happiness and well-being. Love directed toward oneself is the start of growing our love for all beings. Now we can begin to share this feeling with others, those we are close to, and those we are not. Yes, we extend this out even to those who we may not like or for whom we have created some negative feelings toward, such as resentment, anger, or jealousy. These are the best people for us to work with in developing loving-kindness. Although it may not be easy, the key is to find the good in them. We all have Buddha-nature!

2. *Compassion.* The Sanskrit term is *karuna*. The definition is wanting others to be free from suffering. Just as loving-kindness is the wish for the happiness and well-being of oneself and others, the heart of compassion is the wish "May all beings be free of suffering and the causes of suffering." This results in wanting to help others. Helping others reduce their physical or mental suffering is the activity of the Bodhisattva. The ultimate goal is to extinguish suffering by stopping the cause of suffering. The behavior of the Bodhisattva is the constant expression of *bodhichitta* in action.

When watching the news these days, it is difficult to witness the amount of suffering that goes on every day in our world. I know many are said to suffer from compassion fatigue. When we constantly see all forms of suffering on the nightly news, it has a powerful effect. It can make us numb, weary, and emotionally exhausted. Grief is the near enemy of compassion. If we get overwhelmed by emotion, we can succumb to grief. However, it can be an opportunity for us to develop our compassion in these situations.

We do not participate in the actual suffering ourselves. We cultivate compassion. Even for the perpetrator of some terrible atrocities, we can muster a feeling of compassion because we know there will be serious karmic consequences and that individual is going to suffer greatly and for a long time because of their actions.

3. *Sympathetic Joy.* Called *Mudita* in Sanskrit, the definition is rejoicing and being happy for the good fortune of others. By rejoicing in the happiness, success, and good fortune of others and being happy for them, one can actually share in their positive karma.

Sympathetic Joy is an unselfish, positive mental attitude that wishes good fortune for oneself and others. We do this frequently with loved ones, family, and good friends. Watching children play and laugh brings a smile to our face too. This is Sympathetic Joy!

Rejoicing in our virtue underscores our progress on the path. For example, we might take a moment to reflect on our life. If you can bring to mind and recognize the positive changes you have made and are continuing to develop as a result of your practice, take delight in this. This is the practice of Sympathetic Joy.

Do you enjoy seeing others happy and prospering? Do you get jealous when others get the promotion and have success? Practice taking pleasure in the good fortune of others; not only will it make you feel good, but science also tells us it has health benefits too! We will explore those many benefits in a later chapter.

4. *Equanimity. Upekkha* in Sanskrit, this means having a clear, tranquil, and calm state of mind and not being overpowered by delusions, mental dullness, or agitation. With equanimity, we do not distinguish between friend, enemy, or stranger but regard all beings as equal. Equanimity is the basis for unconditional, altruistic love, compassion, and joy for others' happiness. It is the intention and action of cultivating a balanced and even-minded attitude towards all beings, regardless of their status or circumstances.

Practicing equanimity helps us disengage from hopes and fears and shifts the quality of our experience. Consequently, it becomes less likely that we will be pushed and pulled by the vicissitudes of life. We can instead adopt more of an attitude of acceptance and satisfaction. We also can extend this wish to all people—the people in your city, your country, the entire planet, the entire universe, and beyond! "May all beings experience equanimity in their lives." This opening and expansion of our mind and heart is what grows the feeling of equanimity, and our perspective becomes vast.

Practicing the Four Immeasurables involves cultivating and developing these qualities through meditation and daily life. One common method is to begin by directing each quality towards oneself, and then gradually expanding to include loved ones, neutral individuals, and eventually all beings. This can involve visualizing oneself and others as happy, peaceful, and free from suffering, while also cultivating a sense of empathy and compassion toward their struggles and challenges.

This practice is a powerful tool for developing positive emotions and attitudes, as well as for cultivating a greater sense of connection and empathy toward all beings. Through consistent practice, it is believed that these qualities can become more deeply ingrained in one's character, leading to greater happiness, inner peace, and a more compassionate and loving way of being in the world. This is truly an example of Positive Psychology in action.

Give yourself a few minutes to practice this meditation. The result of this practice of equanimity is that our prejudices, strong likes and dislikes, begin to dissolve, and our love, compassion, joy, and equanimity grow. Try it!

Meditation

All Buddhists emphasize meditation, particularly tranquility (*Shamatha*) and insight (*Vipashyana*). These sitting meditation practices differ slightly in different schools but have the same goal—to tame the mind so our Wisdom Mind can shine forth. As mentioned previously, the Buddha's teaching consists of cultivating virtue, avoiding wrongdoing, and taming the mind.

The means for taming the mind is meditation. What follows is a description of the meditation procedure. It is, however, important to have the right view about why we are practicing meditation in the first place. It includes practical and theoretical approaches to our meditation practice, as these two must go together. We need a philosophy to guide our everyday practice. We ultimately change the way we live by positively changing the way we view the world and our place in it.

The Sword of Wisdom
Cuts the clinging to this self,
Awakening Mind!

~ Lama Losang

Guidelines for Shamatha Meditation

Emphasis is placed on the importance of meditation practice. However, we cannot truly practice without some basic understanding of the nature of the mind and reality. The Buddhist teachings guide us in how to become familiar with our basic goodness called Buddha-nature. This is inherent in everyone, without exception.

Our lives have become so complicated and stressful, but we can learn to use our meditation practice to develop calmness and tranquility. It will not bring instant results, but if we are consistent and sincere, beneficial changes will gradually develop.

The basic meditation technique is called calm-abiding or tranquility meditation, *Shamatha* in Sanskrit, or *Shinay* in Tibetan. The word for meditation in Tibetan is *Gom*, and it means "becoming familiar with." We are becoming familiar with our mind. Most of us have not taken the time to look inward and make friends with our mind. We say, "my mind," but what does that mean? That is the meaning of meditation – to directly experience the clear awareness of our mind and rest naturally in that state without the many distractions from our constant mental chatter, known as "monkey mind."

Devote time each day to your meditation practice. Choose a place where you will not be disturbed. The place should be quiet and comfortable. Create a clean, safe, and sacred place for yourself. Some people like to add a flower, incense, a picture of their teacher, or other types of inspirational items that help create a special, sacred environment to enhance beauty and mindful attention.

Shamatha, Tranquility Meditation

Shamatha meditation is a foundational practice in various Buddhist traditions, particularly in the Tibetan Buddhist tradition. The term

Shamatha is derived from the Sanskrit and means "calmness" or "tranquility." The primary objective of Shamatha is to cultivate single-pointed concentration and stability of mind. By training the mind to remain focused on the chosen object of meditation, practitioners develop the ability to sustain attention and reduce distractions. The Buddha taught this to establish basic tranquility and calmness of mind.

As the mind becomes more settled and calm, mental and emotional disturbances begin to subside, leading to a sense of tranquility, clarity, and inner peace. This is essential to progress along the path. Meditation is part of the process of directly experiencing the clear awareness of your mind. Shamatha meditation is considered a foundational practice because it helps to stabilize the mind and develop the necessary concentration for more advanced meditation practices such as *Vipashyana*, Insight Meditation, which we will study next. It is through this focused and calm mind developed in Shamatha that the practitioners gain deeper insights into the nature of reality and the workings of their own minds.

Shamatha meditation is rooted in Buddhist traditions. It has also been adopted and adapted by practitioners of mindfulness and secular meditation. The practice of Shamatha can be beneficial in reducing stress, improving focus, and cultivating a greater sense of well-being and mental balance in daily life.

Calming the mind into a state of peace and tranquility is a prerequisite leading to mindfulness, insight, and wisdom. It affects every experience and how we perceive the world. As one deepens the meditative experience, the mind grows calm and patient, relaxed and at ease, and able to see more clearly. This does not happen without the right effort. We don't see things as *they* are; we see them as *we* are. That way, our happiness is a choice we make.

I will often use the analogy that training our mind is very much like training a puppy. You say, "Stay." Does the puppy listen? If the puppy is like my puppy, she immediately runs off at the slightest distraction. You sit the puppy down and go through this training repeatedly. In training the mind or the puppy, we must start over and over. Getting mad at yourself or the puppy does not help. It is not a matter of force or coercion; you just begin again to tame the mind with patience and perseverance. Training the mind to "stay" is an essential point. The good news is the puppy and our mind are trainable!

'Training the mind to "stay" is essential'

Figure 2: Like a Puppy Can Be Trained, Your Mind Can Be Trained!

Our minds are very powerful. As stated earlier, the Buddha's teaching can be summarized as cultivating excellent virtue, avoiding doing harm and wrongdoing, and totally taming the mind. It is with this understanding that we engage in meditation—to tame the monkey mind.

Meditation is mind training. The following instruction on *Shamatha* requires those practices described when either training our stubborn mind or a distracted puppy. Motivation for cultivating a regular daily practice requires an understanding of the value of meditation and why meditation is important. Once we firmly establish the important place it must take in our life, our progress is assured!

To most beginning students, a meditation on following the breath can seem uninteresting and boring. There is an old story about this. A student once complained to his teacher while sitting on the bank of a river that following the breath was boring. The master grabbed his student and held his head underwater in the river. When the student was released and came up gasping for a breath of air, the master asked, "Did you find the breath boring?" Although a bit harsh, the student would not soon forget that lesson!

Young or old, the length of our life is unknown to each of us. How we spend our time is one of the few real choices we can make. Achieving peace of mind is essential. We all want to be happy and have that peace of mind. We can achieve this with the proper motivation, discipline, and perseverance in our practice.

The Meditation Posture

The proper posture for meditation includes the following five positions. This gives the body the correct and most comfortable sitting position conducive to meditative stability.

Khenpo Rinpoche tells us that there is a difference between the instructions found in the sutras and those in the tantras concerning these positions. The sutric positions are listed below.

1. **Sit comfortably on the floor with your spine straight and legs crossed.** Settle yourself on a comfortable seat in a safe and quiet place, where you will not be disturbed. If you can, sit in the full lotus (*vajra* posture) or in the half lotus posture. In full lotus posture, both feet rest on the opposite thighs with soles upward. If it is too difficult sit in the half lotus, rest one foot on the floor under the leg and bring the other foot up to rest on the opposite thigh. Either position is fine.

You can sit on a small round meditation cushion, called a *zafu*, placed on a *zabuton*, a large square cushion, on the floor. Alternatively, sit on a rolled-up pillow placed on a blanket or large towel on the floor. Another option is to sit toward the edge of a chair with your feet flat on the floor, shoulder-width apart.

Then bring your body to a position of uprightness and a feeling of straightness. If on the floor, sit on the front portion of the cushion with your hips and buttocks about three or four inches above the floor for the best alignment of your spine.

Over time you will find these to be very stable sitting positions. They are referred to as the positions of indestructibility, giving the sense of being well grounded and immovable, like a mountain.

2. **Place your hands in one of the two contemplative gestures.** You can place your hands palm down on your knees. However, this next position is a more traditional position for the hands. Place the back of your right hand in the palm of your left hand with both palms facing up. Your thumbs will be gently touching. Your hands will naturally rest about four finger widths below your navel in your lap and touching your thighs close to your abdomen. In this posture, your thumbs are approximately at the level of your navel. Either of these postures is fine. Find the one that is most comfortable for you.

3. **Keep your spine straight.** Avoid any tendency to lean forward, back, or to the side. Relax the belly and shoulders. Feel you're being gently pulled upward as if by a string on the crown of your head. Make micro-adjustments as needed to maintain straightness throughout your sitting practice. Be gentle and don't strain.

4. **Now we consider the neck, head, and eyes.** The fourth position is with the head straight, gaze down with the eyes at about a forty-five degree angle. The eyes are half-lidded with a gentle and relaxed gaze at an imaginary spot about a foot and a half in front of you. You are not "looking" at anything. Gazing in this way will prevent you from looking up and down or side to side and will help to maintain a relaxed posture and keep the eyes stable.

5. **Chin is slightly tucked in and tip of the tongue is resting on the roof of the mouth.** This helps to straighten the upper cervical vertebrae, aligns the head and neck, and prevents the accumulation of saliva and frequent swallowing. Relax the jaw.

Because some people are not accustomed to these different positions, or because of the difference in flexibility of our bodies and so forth, some of us may be able to do the positions easier and more immediately than others. Whatever the differences, it is important that these positions be understood and that we commit to a daily meditation practice. Correct posture helps the mind find peace, strength, and control. It benefits the physical body by bringing its energies and elements into balance and harmony, creating the conditions for awakening.

For those not able to sit in the above position, you may also sit in a straight-backed chair. Sit toward the edge of the chair and avoid leaning back. Feet are flat on the floor, about shoulder-width apart. Hands are the same as stated above in position 2, either resting on the knees or in the lap.

Experiment with your posture, keeping the back straight, staying relaxed, and observing the other points for your meditation practice as previously stated. As with most things, there is a learning curve. With practice and attention to the posture details, you will soon be able to sit comfortably for extended periods.

Basic Meditation for Taming the Mind

1. **To begin meditation, first, sit in the position described above for a few moments. Then take slow, relaxed, natural breaths.** On the in-breath, imagine the air entering through your nostrils and filling your body all the way down to the level of your navel; on the out-breath, imagine the air going out through the nostrils and down to the level of the floor.

2. **After this initial slow breath, you can stop imagining the breath in this way and just be aware of the sensation in the nostrils.** Be aware of breathing warm air out and cool air in. Then be aware of breathing in and out. When breathing in, be aware of breathing in. When breathing out, be aware of breathing out. Breathe normally. Do not try to make the breath longer or shorter, just let it be natural and uncontrived.

3. **Don't follow distracting thoughts. Follow the breath, which keeps your mind very sharp and clear.** Keep focusing on the sensation of the breath, as this gives the mind something to follow instead of a thought. When breathing in, you're aware of breathing in; and when breathing out, you're aware of breathing out. When you follow the breath out, notice the brief pause or gap at the bottom of the exhale before taking the next breath in. Enjoy that pause of no breath between breaths.

4. **Inevitably, thoughts will distract you now and then, taking you away from your awareness of the breath**. Noticing the distraction is the first benefit you'll experience in meditation. The busyness of the mind is something that has been going on all your life. When you notice that you are involved with a thought, just recognize it as thinking and go back to the sensation of the breath.

There is no judgment about the thoughts, no judgment or blaming yourself if your attention slips. We just continue to mindfully follow the breath. Thoughts come and go; we can imagine them like clouds in a spacious sky or a wave in a vast ocean, seeing the moment of arising and then letting them dissolve back into emptiness. We return again and again to the sensation of breathing, letting the breath anchor our awareness.

Remain mindful and vigilant in the beginning of your practice. We monitor ourselves not to be excessively relaxed or excessively rigid. This balance of correct effort could be compared to a string instrument, such as a lute or guitar. If the strings are too loose and not stretched enough, there'll be no sound, but if stretched too tight, it will break. We want our minds and bodies to be just right, not too loose, not too tight.

In the beginning, try not to entertain any expectation about meditation or its many benefits. Do not think about or focus on acquiring great abilities and powers. Just do the practice without hope and fear and see what happens. Maintain an open and joyful mind. Practice with joyful perseverance.

It is more important to meditate regularly, every day, even if for only a few minutes when practicing meditation. We can begin with mindfully taking twenty-one breaths as our initial step in establishing our daily practice. If we do this for twenty-one days, we will begin the process of constructing a new, lifelong habit of meditation. After twenty-one days you can begin to let go of the counting and just be mindful of naturally riding the wave of your breath and stay present and aware. You can also extend the length of time for your meditation practice and add a second session of practice. We are now strengthening our mental muscle in meditation.

Establishing a Daily Practice

Start by selecting the location for your practice. As in real estate, the three most important things to consider in setting up your meditation space are location, location, and location! A corner in your bedroom or any other quiet spot in your home that is clean, quiet, and gives you a naturally calm feeling will work. You may have to try a couple of spots before finding the right one. You need enough room for your meditation cushion or chair and maybe a little table for your text, a flower, incense, or image that evokes faith and devotion. Create an environment that makes you happy! A space that makes you happy is good feng shui and supports the practice of meditation.

Next, select a time for your practice. I am often asked what the best time is to meditate. The best time to meditate is anytime, day or night. Your daily practice must fit your routines and lifestyle. In the beginning, we must create the habit of sitting. As previously mentioned, if you can be regular and consistent for twenty-one days, you can create a new and lasting habit. Begin by sitting for just twenty-one breaths. When starting to practice, it is better to sit for short periods more frequently. You can extend your sitting time and/or add another session later.

Begin by opening your shrine, which is done by making an offering, such as lighting a candle or offering a flower or incense and making three prostrations. You will often see practitioners doing three prostrations when entering a temple or shrine room. You may wonder what the significance of this is.

In some traditions, it is common to perform three prostrations upon entering a shrine or temple. This practice is rooted in the idea of showing respect, humility, and devotion, in this case, to the Buddha, the Dharma, and the Sangha. By performing three prostrations, a practitioner is expressing their reverence toward these three important aspects of the path. In addition, prostrations also can be seen as a form of physical and mental purification. By bowing and touching the ground with five points, the forehead, hands, and knees, a practitioner is symbolically offering their body, speech, and mind to the Three Jewels, and letting go of their attachments, ego, and delusions. Consequently, this can also be a way of generating merit, which leads to spiritual progress and liberation.

If you cannot do three prostrations with the five points on the ground as mentioned, bow from the waist three times with the same aspiration and intention stated above.

Take your seat as described with seven points. Cultivate the mind of enlightenment, *bodhichitta*, the wish to attain enlightenment motivated by great compassion for all sentient beings. This is accompanied by a falling away of the attachment to the illusion of an inherently existing self.

Take a couple of deep breaths and relax. Breathe in through the nostrils and out through the mouth, completely exhausting all the old, stale air. After a few cleansing breaths, bring your awareness to the breath and breathe through the nose. Breathe naturally. Feel the breath at the nostrils, cool on the inhale, warm on the exhale, chest and belly gently expanding and contracting with the breath.

Imagine your mind spacious like the sky and the thoughts that come into your awareness are like clouds in that vast sky. See the arising of a thought, and instead of following or encouraging it, let it dissolve into emptiness like the clouds in the sky. Be careful not to judge the thoughts as they arise, as this is just another distracting thought. Thoughts are neither good nor bad, just the play of the mind. Your anchor is the breath. Return to it again and again, like training our puppy, with not only love and patience but also awareness and perseverance. Remember to be gentle with yourself.

When breathing in, be aware of the sensations of breathing in. When breathing out, ride the natural wave of the breath to the end before taking the next breath. Notice any pause at the top of the inhale or the bottom of the exhale. *Be the breath.*

The breath may naturally slow down. We are not forcibly trying to slow the breath down. As we relax more and more, you may find your breath slowing down over time, to about four or five breaths per minute. You are not in a rush, so please be at ease. Gently, and with awareness, continue to ride the wave of your breath. Keep a light heart and the feeling of gratitude for the freedom to practice. Feel the natural peace, tranquility, and clarity of the mind. Enjoy this time!

Summary of *Shamatha* Meditation Instruction

As a review, it is beneficial to have the eyes slightly open, half-lidded, allowing in a little light—not closed nor fully open as we usually do. Eyes are gently opened, unfocused and relaxed, gazing downward without strain at an imaginary spot about two feet in front and at a forty-five-degree angle down.

Let your awareness come to the breath. When breathing in, be aware of breathing in. When breathing out, be aware of breathing out. Let the breath be natural and uncontrived. Do not intentionally try to speed it up or slow it down; simply stay present and ride the wave of your breath. Continue to follow the breath and be aware of distractions, thoughts, feelings, and emotions that can take you away from staying in the present. You can rest briefly in the gap between the out-breath and the next in-breath.

Watch for projections into the future or reflection on the past. Stay present! We tend to be time travelers. We are constantly reflecting on the past or projecting into some future world we are constantly creating. Rarely are we resting in the precious present moment, free of the tyranny of our subjective mind pushing and pulling us in all directions.

This constant barrage of mental chatter requires a great deal of energy to maintain – no wonder we are exhausted at the end of the day. Fortunately, there is something we can do to bring sanity into our lives! It is great if you can find a meditation center with a qualified and knowledgeable teacher with whom you can study and get questions answered. However, this isn't always possible. If you follow these instructions and persevere with diligence, you will find it to be of great benefit.

To summarize, the Buddha taught six different aspects of *Shamatha* meditation. These are (1) have the correct posture, (2) hold the mind on the breath, (3) cut the stream of thoughts and mental chatter, (4) eliminate dullness and agitation, (5) the mind is not too tight or too loose, and (6) let the mind be at ease and maintain awareness of the breath. I've listed some helpful reminders on how to achieve these below.

Physical Posture:

1. Take a stable seat.
2. Place the hands.
3. Straighten the spine.
4. Tuck in the chin.
5. Tongue on the roof of the mouth.
6. Lower the gaze.

Mental Attention:

1. Place awareness on the breath.
2. Follow the in-breath and out-breath.
3. Initially begin by silently counting each out-breath twenty-one times. Then let go of the counting and mindfully follow the breath.

When Attention Wanders:

1. Notice the distraction as it arises.
2. Label the distraction "thinking."
3. Let go of the distraction.
4. Return your attention to the breath.

Mind Is Not Too Tight:

1. Body and mind are relaxed and at ease.

2. No strain or forcing attention.
3. Mind is vast, like space, and free of stress.

Mind Is Not Too Loose:

1. Mind is clear and free of dullness.
2. Notice any distraction as it arises.
3. Be mindful, remain present, and ride the wave of your breath.

Shamatha and Vipashyana Meditation

The two ways through which we can gain freedom from our habitual mental and emotional patterns both involve meditation. In our meditation practice, we work with our body, speech, and mind. But of these three, the mind is the most important. This attention to the mind is called mindfulness. It is the awareness of this present moment, what is happening right now. Through these practices, we are training our minds to live in the ever-present now. With a mind that is relaxed and at ease, we can become aware of this precious moment. With this awareness, we consequently notice when our mind is wandering and distracted and can then gently return to the present. This is working with our inner puppy. Remember, we are trainable!

As previously discussed, we gain more mental stability and calmness through the *Shamatha*, tranquility meditation, which leads to fewer thoughts and less agitation. The mind becomes workable, stable, and unmoving. We are developing our mental muscle. However, this does not uproot the prime cause of suffering: the identification with this ego image of a self. We now are ready to begin the second process, insight meditation, which entails a systematic analysis to deconstruct this manufactured "self," this "I" to which we are so attached. In Sanskrit, it is called *Vipashyana*, and in Tibetan, *Lhaktong*. The two types of meditation work beautifully together, and each are indispensable to our progress on the path.

Vipashyana, **Insight Meditation**

Vipashyana (Sanskrit) is also called *Vipassana* (Pali) and means a "clear insight" or "seeing deeply" into the nature of reality. It too is practiced in various forms across different Buddhist schools and has gained popularity outside of Buddhism as a secular mindfulness practice. Only after we have sufficiently developed a strong tranquility meditation and have quieted the mind and made it workable, can we use it for Vipashyana insight meditation.

When the mind is stable, we can say "stay" and our mind is trained and capable of doing so. We now have established a mind at ease when resting or engaged. We can now rest in the natural mind where deeper insights flow forth, undisturbed by the workings of the previously untamed mind. We have uprooted the causes of our suffering, the clinging and attachment to a contrived self with which we have become so identified. Vipashyana frees us from mental obscurations that cloud the mind and obstruct our seeing the mind's true nature. We can deepen and remain in meditative absorption, *samadhi*, for extended periods of time.

The aim is to cultivate insight into emptiness, impermanence, and the selfless nature of all phenomena. Vipashyana is to be experienced; it's non-conceptual. This leads to the further development of wisdom, compassion, and liberation from suffering. Through direct experiential insights, practitioners may come to realize the impermanent and conditioned nature of all phenomena, thereby reducing attachment, aversion, and ignorance. It is important to understand that Vipashyana meditation is a profound and multifaceted practice that is best learned and practiced under the guidance of an experienced teacher, or within a structured retreat setting.

At the conclusion of your practice, Dedicate the Merit with a brief prayer, offering the virtue of your practice for the benefit of all beings. This concludes your practice.

This is the foundation upon which all other practices can be built. Like building a house, we must first build a strong foundation upon which the house can stand.

Walking Meditation

The Buddha said to practice mindfulness while in all four postures and all activities. In meditation retreats around the world, yogis practice mindfulness when walking, standing, sitting, and lying down. They practice mindfulness at all times and in all situations.

We can do walking meditation at any time, by itself or in conjunction with our sitting practice. During walking meditation, there is no visualization. When you are walking, *know* you're walking. This is the meaning of terms such as mindfulness and awareness and thus is another skillful means for enhancing mindfulness.

Walk as if you are kissing the Earth with your feet.

~Thich Nhat Hanh

It was the Buddha himself who first taught the walking meditation found in the great discourse on *The Foundations of Mindfulness*. Now people are not used to sitting in meditation for an extended period. They may feel agitated and are bothered by pain or become dull, lethargic, and sleepy. Instead of stopping your meditation, it is better to do a combination of sitting and walking practice. The movement of walking meditation helps wake us up and improves the clarity of the mind by improving the circulation of Chi and blood. Chi is the vital energetic life force of the body, which we will explore more as we progress in our studies in *Book 2: Tai Chi/Chi Gong: Exercises for Health and Longevity.*

One other important reason for walking meditation is that it helps with post-meditation. We can bring our meditation experience to our daily life as we move and go about our daily activities but without leaving the meditative mindset of peace and tranquility on our meditation cushion. This takes you closer to bringing meditation or some sense of meditative momentum into your day-to-day life. This bridging between formal and informal practice is an important step.

Instruction for Walking Meditation

1. **Hands.** We hold the hands in front at the level of the navel, with the palms up and the right hand on top of the left. Let the tip of the thumbs gently touch, similar to the sitting practice. This is a gesture of mindfulness and equipoise.

2. **Feet.** We walk by first lifting the heel upward, rolling the foot forward toward the tip of the toe, and then lifting the foot off the ground and moving it forward, taking the step and placing the heel on the ground first and gradually the whole foot.

3. **Be Mindful of These Four Stages.** There are various stages of walking meditation as one progresses in this practice of mindfulness meditation. This way, we take moderate steps with the right foot first and walk in a straight line or a clockwise circle. You are instructed to be mindful of only one thing during walking meditation—the act of stepping in four stages.

   1. Lifting the foot.
   2. Moving the foot forward.
   3. Putting the foot down.

4. Shifting the weight and pressing the foot on the ground.

Remain present and make a mental note of these four stages of the foot's movement by internally repeating "lifting, moving forward, putting down, and pressing the ground" as you shift the weight.

4. **Pace.** Walk at a slower speed than normal during this practice, and as your experience grows, you can observe more and more the different stages of each step. By practicing this regularly, you will experience all movements clearly and distinctly and become more mindful and aware. This contributes to our cultivation of mindfulness.

Before beginning this practice of walking meditation, you may have thought that a step is just one movement. While engaged in this meditation on walking, observe these four movements. Mind and matter and the arising and disappearing of all phenomena are all examples of constant change and impermanence.

Modern physicists know this very well. They have observed with powerful instruments that matter is just a constantly changing vibration of particles and energy. There is nothing substantial to any of it. By realizing the nature of impermanence, yogis and scientists understand there is really nothing to hold on to in the entire world of phenomena.

This practice is helpful in contributing toward a more wholesome and tranquil state of the mind. Your mind is focused on lifting, moving, setting your foot down, and pressing against the ground, then shifting the weight from leg to leg and repeating the procedure. We are cultivating mindful awareness with every step!

Four

The Six Perfections: Cultivating Virtue

ℬ ℬ ℬ ⎯⎯⎯⎯⎯⎯⎯⎯⎯⎯⎯⎯⎯⎯⎯⎯⎯⎯⎯⎯⎯⎯

We all are faced with a question that life imposes upon us. This question is at the heart of all philosophies, and its answer determines every action we take. We may ask ourselves using different words, but the core query is: *What kind of a person do I want to be?* This goes beyond all the labels and the initials after our names and all the titles we accumulate. Some people intentionally and conscientiously endeavor to cultivate virtuous qualities, while others just follow their impulses and desires. These decisions create very different results and life paths.

We return again to the three primary principles taught by the Buddha in cultivating the mind of enlightenment. Simply put, these three are:

1. Cultivate virtue in abundance.
2. Avoid doing harm to oneself and to others.
3. Completely tame your mind.

On the path to enlightenment, we endeavor to practice and apply the skillful methods taught by the sages and saints down through the ages. They all speak of developing the kind of life we want through the joyful perseverance of self-cultivation. We will focus on a very practical, deliberate, and intentional method to practice and develop what is known as the Six Perfections; they also can be called the Six Paramitas or the Six Virtues. This is the way to cultivate virtue.

Six Perfections (*Paramitas*): Qualities for Self-Transformation

These Six Perfections are found in the early Mahayana sutras and will be the basis of our book's meditations on self-cultivation. A meditation is associated with each of the Six Perfections: Generosity, Ethics, Patience, Joyous Effort, Concentration, and Wisdom. The cultivation of the perfection of each of these six virtuous qualities of human character guides an individual toward the goal of realizing the mind of enlightenment. In all authentic spiritual traditions, the aspiration to arouse and engender this enlightened mind for the benefit of all beings guides their practice. The practitioner's motivation to practice virtue makes greater insight and greater freedom possible.

We are shaped by many different factors as we grow our sense of who we are. Our genetics, parents, family, social, economic, and many other forces impact and shape our identity. However, these do not influence us as strongly as the deliberate choices we make for ourselves. These conscious decisions made every day over time are instrumental in cultivating our moral character. They are continually building our character for better or worse and even influencing our overall health.

Let's put this idea into the proper context. This cultivation of virtue is more like continuous training flowing throughout our lives rather than a rigid set of principles and rules. We could say that our first "awakening" in life is the direct realization that we alone are responsible for our progress on the path to self-transformation. It is *our* responsibility – no one can do it for us! It is at this moment we begin to generate the thought of self-cultivation.

When we recognize that we are responsible for our destiny, we take our first intentional step on our spiritual path. Prior to this realization, we are blown like a leaf in the wind without a guiding principle for our day-to-day activities. This view of engendering the thought of enlightenment opens us to heightened mindfulness and awareness.

We can compare this to the discipline required to maintain our physical fitness, which is accomplished by paying attention to our diet, sleep, exercise, etc. In cultivating our character and moral fitness, we also need to concentrate on certain behaviors. To succeed at either of these pursuits for any prolonged period, we will need a joyful and diligent attitude.

The way you do this will be very particular to you, your environment, lifestyle, working conditions, family, and overall health because you are unique in the world. *There is no one like you now, nor has there ever been, nor will there ever be a person like you.* The causes and conditions that brought you into this world and set the stage for your development are unique to precious you. Therefore, how you navigate the various experiences in your life also will be your responsibility that requires mindfulness and attention.

We all come into this world with our own set of preceding causes and conditions, strengths and weaknesses, hopes and fears to be worked through. The following Six Perfections shine like the sun, illuminating every step along your path.

1. Perfect Generosity

This is the perfect enlightened quality of charity and giving. The essence of this virtue is unconditional love, a boundless openness of heart and mind. It is giving freely without expectation, free of attachment and of getting something in return. There are three kinds of generosity for us to consider: (1) giving material help to those who lack the material necessities of life, (2) giving protection to those in fear, and (3) giving pure Dharma teachings to those who request them.

The giving of material help can include giving to charity, the homeless, friends in need, famine and disaster victims, organizations that feed the poor or support animal shelters, or any type of place offering protection, comfort, and health services. There are many other opportunities to give protection to those who live in fear. Supporting these organizations and charities in any form can provide much relief. We give according to our capacity without remorse or regret.

When it comes to giving Dharma teachings, we may feel it is beyond our capacity. In some ways, this is true, but the essence of Dharma is simple kindness and compassion toward others. It is having a loving heart.

There are many different intentions for and ways of giving. Thus, we must be mindful of our motivation when giving, even when it's sharing teachings or information. We can give with an impure motivation, such as to make ourselves look good or to get credit and praise for our good actions, to be well thought of or held in esteem, or to get something in return. This is not pure giving because it is conditional.

Being mindful of what we give and its result is also good to reflect upon. For example, considering that gifts of alcohol, tobacco, drugs, or weapons may have some immediate, short-term benefit but can be detrimental in the long run.

Giving is one of the most essential preliminary steps of our practice, and that is why it comes first. It should always be unconditional and free of selfish desires for gratitude, recognition, advantage, or reputation. True generosity is not accomplished by the action of giving nor by the gift itself, but by having pure motivation.

To cultivate generosity, it's wise to contemplate not only the benefits of this practice but also the disadvantages of being miserly. It's also wise to reflect on the obvious fact that our bodies and our wealth are impermanent. Generosity is a cure for the afflictions of greed, miserliness, and possessiveness. In this practice of giving, we may offer our time, energy, money, food, clothing, or gifts to assist others. This is done naturally and selflessly, without a cost/benefit analysis!

Generosity Meditation

When freely and skillfully given, forgiveness demonstrates the Perfection of Generosity. Forgiveness means different things to different people. It can involve the intentional decision to let go of resentment and anger toward another or yourself.

The action that hurt or offended you may still carry some emotional charge. But working on forgiveness can help lessen the grip it has on you. It can help us let go of the control that another person or situation has over you and give you the ability to gain true freedom from that resentment and anger. Letting go of those old grudges and bitterness can actually improve your health and peace of mind when seen as an act of generosity. Forgiveness can lead to healthier relationships, improved health, less anxiety, a stronger immune system, increased self-esteem, and even lower blood pressure!

Forgiveness can be difficult. If you find yourself stuck, try the following:

1. *Sit comfortably in a quiet environment.* Let your awareness come to the breath and take a few relaxed breaths.

2. *When you're ready, make the decision to forgive.* Deciding to forgive involves coming to terms with the situation and freeing yourself from the chains that keep you bound. What you will be doing as you forgive is generously extending an act of love toward the person who has hurt you. When we offer this love, we deliberately reduce the resentment and the persistent ill will toward this person. Instead, we offer them kindness, respect, generosity, and love.

3. *It is important to emphasize that forgiveness does not involve excusing the person's actions, forgetting what happened, or tossing justice aside.* It is an opportunity to develop our loving-kindness and compassion. It is part of our mind-training.

Follow the guidelines below for the tranquility meditation to enhance forgiveness. Remember, as with all our meditations, we begin by generating *bodhichitta*.

1. ***Begin by finding a quiet place and take a comfortable seat.*** Always begin with taking a few breaths as when doing the tranquility meditation. Settle your mind and relax.

2. ***We start with a question.*** Ask yourself this question about the person who has hurt you. Do you know what life was like for this person growing up, or what it is like for them now? We may not be aware of the difficulties they may have had growing up or recently. Some people have difficulty handling stress and act out because of fear or confusion. There are always causes and conditions that influence behavior. These questions are not meant to excuse or condone but rather to better understand another's pain and what makes them vulnerable and stressed.

3. ***Be aware of the thoughts and feelings that may be arising and let them dissolve into emptiness, naturally self-liberated.*** They come and go, and we watch with equanimity and without judgment. Are you aware of a slight welling up of compassion and loving-kindness toward the person who offended you? Nourish this feeling, like caring and protecting a seedling's tender shoot pushing up in our spring garden. We can see the situation with new eyes. The person may have been confused, mistaken, and misguided. They may even deeply regret their actions. As you think about this person, be aware of a softer feeling growing in your heart toward them and expand that positive feeling of caring, empathy, and compassion.

4. ***As we return to the breath, we dedicate the merit of this meditation*** for the benefit of all beings and to help them find the generous heart of forgiveness.

2. Perfect Ethics or Morality

This is the perfect enlightened quality of virtuous and ethical behavior, morality, self-discipline, personal integrity, honor, and harmlessness. The essence of this virtue is that through our love and compassion, we do not harm others with our thoughts, speech, or actions. Practicing the perfection of ethics is being mindful and refraining from the ten non-virtuous actions that are grouped into similar types. The *four of speech*: telling lies, slandering others, gossiping, and using harsh speech and swearing. The *three non-virtues of the body*: killing, stealing, and sexual misconduct. The *three of the mind*: craving and attachment, wishing to harm others, and holding wrong views.

I like the analogy of cultivating our minds and growing our garden. We must do two things. We prepare the ground and plant the flowers and plants we wish to cultivate and give them what they need to grow strong. We also uproot and pull out the weeds that can overcome and compete with our desired harvest. Likewise, the cultivation of morality and ethics includes nurturing good qualities as well as uprooting negative behaviors. We continue to develop loving-kindness and compassion for others as well as not harming them, trying to expand our goodwill toward all beings.

When our mind is free from negative emotions, it naturally becomes tranquil and focused, and our loving-kindness and compassion will arise naturally. It is unlikely that we can practice pure morality in all things at the beginning of our practice; however, we can develop these good qualities and refrain from expressing negative emotions.

These guidelines are in no way meant to be a burden or restriction on our freedom. We follow these precepts so we can enjoy greater freedom, happiness, and security in our lives because, through our virtuous behavior, we are no longer creating conditions for suffering in the future. We will come to realize that unethical behavior is always a cause of suffering and unhappiness.

Practicing the virtue of ethics, we are free of negativity; we are at ease, naturally confident, and happy because we are not carrying any underlying sense of guilt or remorse. We have nothing to hide. Maintaining our integrity and upright moral conduct is the cause of all goodness, happiness, and ultimate freedom.

Ethics Meditation:

1. *Take a few minutes to contemplate.* Focus on the meaning of ethical and moral behavior in your life.
2. *Consider the advantages of cultivating ethical behavior and the disadvantages of unethical behavior.* In so doing, we will develop great enthusiasm for this practice of ethics.
3. *Consider the consequences of unethical behavior.* Practicing the Perfection of Ethics, we are free of negativity, we cause no harm to others by our actions, our speech is kind and compassionate, and we are at ease, confident, and without stress. We can relax.

3. Perfect Patience

Perfect Patience is the enlightened realization of tolerance, forbearance, and acceptance. Its essence is the strength of mind and heart that enables us to face life's challenges and difficulties without losing our composure and inner tranquility. We cannot accomplish anything without patience.

The ability to endure, to have forbearance, is critical to our practice. We have the capacity to remain loving and compassionate even in the face of aggression and conflict. Practicing patience gives us great inner strength and courage to face difficult situations. We are less likely to get upset when things don't go our way and less likely to act badly toward others. It creates a little space for equanimity and an opportunity to disengage and take a breath before responding.

Patience also can be called forbearance and gives us the capacity for forgiveness and to accept suffering. It prevents us from getting angry if someone mistreats us, which usually only aggravates the situation. Instead of mindlessly reacting, we realize the person giving us a difficult time is suffering and out of control. It creates the conditions for compassion toward that individual, and we don't have to behave in the same aggressive or unskillful way. We remain calm and, hopefully, in that way, are able to diffuse the situation so it can be resolved calmly. We do our best to embrace adversity, insult, distress, and the wrongs of others with patience and tolerance, free of resentment, irritation, and emotional reactivity.

In practicing this virtue, we never give up on or abandon others. We help them cross over the sea of suffering. We maintain our inner peace and maintain calmness and equanimity.

Patience Meditation

When we see the rising of anger in ourselves, we can transform it with patience. Patience is the antidote to anger. A Bodhisattva practices patience as a skillful means not to allow people or circumstances to dictate their state of mind. The following guided meditation may be practiced:

1. *Begin by bringing your attention to your breath.* Take a few slow, deep breaths, and relax. Let go of any thoughts and emotions, and let your breath be natural and at ease. Continue to gently ride the natural wave of your breath without trying to control it in any way.

2. *Now think of irritating thoughts you may have experienced such as tasks that remain unfinished, or of someone who may have upset you.* All of these are just the play of the mind. You can remain at ease, choosing in this moment not to engage with the irritating thoughts and choose to remain calm in the present

moment. Let yourself feel the spaciousness of your mind, the power of the feeling of stillness. You remain relaxed and calm. This is the power of patience.

3. ***Now think of a time when you were impatient, angry, and upset.*** It may have been a heated argument with a loved one, or out in public with a stranger, or even privately getting upset and irritated with yourself. Feel that energy, feeling the heart rate increase, blood pressure rising, tempers flaring, and getting hot and bothered.

4. ***Compare that feeling with the feeling of calm and patience.*** Which of those qualities should we abandon, and which should we cultivate?

5. ***Breathe in that spacious quality of love, compassion, and equanimity when you breathe in.*** When you breathe out, let go of any impatience, irritation, frustration, and agitation.

6. ***Breathe in openness, calmness, and lightness.*** Fill your body with natural ease and peace of mind.

7. ***Return to the breath and Dedicate the Merit*** that all beings may benefit by the cultivation of patience.

4. Perfect Joyous Effort

Joyous Effort is the perfection of the enlightened quality of energy, vigor, vitality, endurance, diligence, enthusiasm, and persistent effort. The essence of Joyful Effort is having the courage, energy, and endurance to untiringly benefit others without expecting personal recognition or reward.

To practice the first three Perfections of Generosity, Ethics or Morality, and Patience in the face of difficulties, we need the Perfection of Joyous Effort and Perseverance. This gives us the energy and endurance to continuously practice the Dharma and pursue our goal of enlightenment for the good of all beings. To continue when things get tough, this quality of joyful effort and enthusiastic perseverance is needed. This is our attitude toward our spiritual practice. We will come to appreciate and have great joy at having found such a wonderful way of life. This virtue has three aspects:

1. Understanding the great value of traveling the path and having full confidence that we can do it.

2. Maintaining our joyful effort despite setbacks we might encounter along the way. For example, we need the determination and perseverance to be consistent in meditation practice when we feel burdened by our daily responsibilities.

3. Persevering in our journey until we arrive at the destination. I previously stated the two obstacles on the path to freedom. They are not starting, and if started, not continuing to the end. Once we have entered the path to freedom, we maintain our positive attitude to go all the way to its completion.

When we practice this type of diligence and perseverance, we also cultivate a strong and healthy mind. Joyous Effort gives us great determination for achieving any of our goals, even when facing obstacles or problems. Not giving up is essential to the success of any endeavor. We are developing our mental muscles!

Joyous Effort Meditation:

1. *Sit comfortably in a quiet place, where you can be free from distractions and disturbances.* Breathe slowly and steadily through the nose, and let the breath be natural and relaxed.

2. *Invite the feeling of joy into your heart by contemplating the importance of having this positive attitude toward our meditation practice.* We are practicing for a twofold benefit: for ourselves and for others. Our practice becomes imbued with joy

and ease. Allow a deep feeling of satisfaction to arise as you apply Joyful Effort.

3. *You may begin to contemplate the benefits you've already received through the practice of mindfulness in meditation, loving-kindness, and compassion.* This brings a feeling of gratitude.

4. *Dedicate the Merit of this practice to all beings.* May all beings experience Joyful Effort for the practice of Dharma.

5. Perfect Concentration

Perfect Concentration is the enlightened quality of meditation, contemplation, mindfulness, and mental stability.

Our minds have the tendency to be very distracted and restless, always moving from one thought or feeling to another. If we don't stabilize the mind with meditative concentration to quiet our restless mind, we will just keep engaging in the same habitual patterns of thought and behavior. Remember: training our puppy to stay is not an easy task. However, it is important for both you and the puppy!

Meditation makes our minds trainable and workable. There is no attainment of wisdom without developing our mind through the regular practice of *Shamatha* for stability in meditation. With the same enthusiasm that we may go to the gym and work out to cultivate our physical strength, we practice taming the mind in meditation to cultivate our mental strength.

When we train our mind by practicing meditation, such as the *Shamatha* and *Vipashyana* meditation practices, we achieve attention, clarity, composure, and tranquility. This helps us be present in our lives and to overcome stress and anxiety.

The development of undistracted concentration requires perseverance, attention, mindfulness, and awareness—but the rewards are worth it!

Concentration Meditation: *Shamatha* and *Vipashyana*

The essence of concentration is the cultivation of our *Shamatha* and *Vipashyana* practices. Persevere in these meditation practices daily. Remember the Tibetan word for meditation is *gom* and it means "becoming familiar with." We are becoming more and more familiar with our mind's true nature. This continuous deepening of our meditative absorption is essential for progress on our path to enlightenment. For details on this meditation please review *Chapter 3: Meditation*.

6. Perfect Wisdom

Perfect Wisdom is the culmination of the previous five Perfections. It is the quality of transcendent wisdom, insight, and understanding. It also is the hardest for us to realize because of habitual patterns that obscure our mind's true nature. Perfect Wisdom is the highest understanding and realization that human beings can attain. It is the perfected enlightened quality of insight and total clarity.

Also, with this Perfect Wisdom we are better able to cultivate the other five Perfections: Generosity, Ethics or Morality, Patience, Joyous Effort, and Concentration. It is the awakened wisdom that realizes the interdependent nature of all things. We see the essential nature of reality with profound lucidity. Our perception soars beyond the illusive and deceptive veils of material existence. We release our ego attachment and dissolve all dualistic concepts with this insight. While practicing the first five virtues to develop wisdom, we are also practicing wisdom by letting go of our ego-clinging and self-absorption.

Wisdom Meditation:

Wisdom meditation is the essence of our spiritual journey. As previously stated, insight meditation leads to the direct realization of emptiness. Emptiness cannot be seen as a thing, an object of meditation, as relating to it in this way only results in a conceptual understanding. The luminous clarity of the mind must be experienced directly. It goes beyond the duality of a perceiver and that which is perceived.

With the correct view, we come to understand that emptiness and the arising of disturbing thoughts and conflicting emotions are not separate. We allow these experiences to arise in the mind.

When thoughts, feelings and emotions arise, pay attention to where they come from. When they persist, try to establish where they are. After they dissolve, pay attention to the mental clarity that is present in the mind even when no thoughts, feelings, or emotions are to be found.

With mindfulness and awareness, we see how these thoughts and emotions are naturally self-liberated into emptiness. Notice the luminous clarity of the mind. This is the practice of insight meditation that leads to the realization of our Buddha-nature.

The exercises found in the next two chapters will facilitate the cultivation of Wisdom and Compassion. Take time to become familiar with each practice. We will start with *Tonglen*.

Five

Tonglen: Cultivating Compassion

ॐ ॐ ॐ ⎯⎯⎯⎯⎯⎯⎯⎯⎯⎯⎯⎯⎯⎯⎯⎯

T he Bodhisattva Sutra says, "Give yourself to others" and contains stories of how the Bodhisattvas, Buddhas in training, gave everything to benefit others. But we are not being asked to give blindly; we give out of the kindness of an open and loving heart.

To get to the highest level of giving, we must first learn how to give as we talked about in our discussion on Perfect Generosity. We make a habit of letting go and detaching from self-clinging. The main practice for developing this "letting go" is called *Tonglen*. This ancient form of meditation focuses on compassion: connecting with it, developing it, and learning how to apply it in everyday life. Sometimes it is called "Exchanging Self for Other."

The practice of *Tonglen* is very simple. We imagine that as we are exhaling, we are sharing our happiness, love, health, compassion, and their causes with everyone. As we inhale, we imagine taking away their suffering and the causes of suffering in all its myriad forms.

While its roots are Buddhist, in recent years, *Tonglen* meditation has found receptive audiences from spiritual to therapeutic to secular. Its popularity is surprising, given how different it is from the usual focus of our "me first" society. As it turns out, the most powerful ways to be kind to yourself and create the causes of happiness in the future are by developing the strong intention and the motivation to help others. People from all walks of life have found it beneficial.

The word *Tonglen* is a Tibetan term that translates as "sending and taking." The practice belongs to a great body of wisdom called *Lojong* in Tibetan. *Lo* means "mind," and *jong* means "training." This Mind Training is considered one of the most important teachings in Buddhism. *Tonglen* is a special application of the Mind Training practice. It is a skillful means to cultivate *bodhichitta* and learn how to be less self-centered and selfish. Our meditation trains the mind to be more loving and compassionate.

In addition to an intellectual understanding of *bodhichitta* from the teachings, it is important to cultivate the experience directly. The following exercises will help give birth to *bodhichitta*, the mind of enlightenment.

Tonglen Meditation Overview

Tonglen practice begins with breath awareness and continues with the wish to establish all beings in happiness and free from suffering. It is an easy meditation to say, but not always so easy to do.

There are many different versions of this practice, traditional and modern. The simplest form is simply connecting your motivation and breath. As you inhale, you breathe in the discomfort, unhappiness, pain, distress, and their causes. You imagine that when you exhale, you share the light of happiness, health, well-being, and their causes. Soothing rays of healing light fill the entire world with their benevolent healing power on the out-breath. When breathing in, imagine you are breathing in a dark, smoky-like cloud representing the suffering of sentient beings. The darkness is transformed by your positive intention and the natural goodness of your heart. Then send out healing, love, compassion, and all that is needed and wanted in the form of brilliant light that enters the person or people, making them very happy and satisfying all their needs.

Tonglen is often practiced in stages. After settling the mind in meditation, we choose an object of compassion: a person, animal, or group. We breathe in the smoky darkness of that specific distress, imagining the object of our meditation is relieved of all difficulties, whatever they may be. We breathe out the soothing light of compassion; it touches the object of compassion, bringing comfort and peace. This is followed by a phase of expanding the visualization to others who experienced similar distress and expanding yet out again to the farthest reaches of the multiverse until all suffering is alleviated and all goodness is shared with all beings.

Tonglen minimizes and gradually uproots the conflicting emotions of our self-clinging and engages us physically, mentally, emotionally, and verbally in developing tolerance, patience, compassion, and loving-kindness. The renowned teacher Khenpo Karthar Rinpoche explains it this way: "Enlightened beings have reached enlightenment by working for the benefit of all sentient beings. Beings remain in samsara (suffering) because they are working for themselves alone."

By letting go of selfishness, we work to benefit others rather than working merely to benefit ourselves. This altruistic attitude is the source of future happiness.

Tonglen Meditation Practice:

1. *Sit comfortably.*

2. *Begin with Shamatha meditation, maintaining your awareness of the breath.* As you breathe in, be present and aware that you are breathing in. As you breathe out, be aware of the breathing-out. Be mindful of any distracting thoughts and emotions; as soon as they arise, let them go and return to the breath.

3. *Now link your intention to the breath.* On the exhale, breathe out the light of your basic goodness and wish to benefit suffering beings, and with that, you alleviate pain and suffering by sending out loving-kindness and compassion. Breathe in the smoky darkness of unhappiness and suffering in all its myriad forms into

your heart, where it is transformed into light. ***Do this sequence three, six, or nine times.***

4. ***Extend your meditation to others who are scared, fearful, and agitated.*** Breathe in their distress and breathe out happiness and peace. Imagine their distress is resolved.

5. ***Expand this goodwill and imagine it reaching the far limits of space.*** We are only limited by the scope of our imagination and motivation. Allow your heart and natural goodness to shine unreservedly and touch the world with its blessing of love, compassion, and wisdom.

For example, when I was flying recently, there was a mother and her young child in the aisle across from me. We were about to take off, and the child was frightened, anxious, and crying. The mother was trying her best to calm the child without much success and was becoming frustrated and irritated. In this situation, I began doing *Tonglen* meditation, inhaling the fear, panic, and anxiety the child was feeling and the irritation the mother was experiencing, and breathing out calm, serenity, and tranquility to both. The child almost immediately began to calm down, and consequently, so did the mother. I can't say it always works like that, but it certainly seemed to bring peace and ease to the mother and child. I have done this on numerous occasions with good results. My method for this was as follows:

1. ***Begin by connecting with the breath.*** Taking a breath in, imagine breathing in her fear, distress, anxiety, agitation, and frustration. While doing so, feel she is being relieved of her suffering and distress.

2. ***Now breathing out soothing, gentle light that reassures and comforts her.*** Imagine that she feels safe, loved, and cared for, repeating this sequence until the energy shifts and calm returns.

3. ***Next, expanding the meditation to her mother, the other passengers on the plane, and eventually to all others who were***

scared, fearful, irritated, and agitated. Breathing in their distress and breathing out happiness, love and peace of mind. Imagine their distress is completely resolved and well-being is restored.

4. *Extending this goodwill, love and peace, imagining it covers and envelops the entire country, then to all countries, nations and people of the world. Imagine it extending further and further, beyond the limits of space.* With this last step we feel increasingly connected to everyone with deepening peace, love, and compassion. This becomes a heartfelt blessing to the grand infinity, expanding love and compassion to the farthest reaches of space.

Tonglen is not just for when you are sitting in meditation; it also can be a part of your life wherever you go and whatever you are doing. You can offer any activity for the benefit of others, at work, at home, while eating or engaged in any activity. For example, when you are taking a walk, review this thought in your mind: "May all beings experience happiness." When you inhale, think, "May all beings be relieved of suffering," and when you exhale, think, "May I give others comfort and happiness."

This becomes a natural expression of the mind of enlightenment. You can practice Tonglen with every breath you take. This attitude takes time to develop as it goes against our old habits and tendencies to think only of ourselves and our happiness. This is the training of a Bodhisattva and the essence of the Mahayana path.

When training the mind as beginners, we will still have disturbing thoughts. Our Tonglen and other practices will help us learn how to handle them. How can we practice this? We must apply mindfulness. For example, the moment we are aware that we are experiencing anger or another conflicting emotion, we can think, "May my experience of this anger be transformed to benefit all sentient beings, and may all sentient beings be free of that disturbing emotion."

The emotion itself is not positive, but the way you have handled it *is* positive. This skillful means helps to foster positive feelings and to think of the welfare of others.

Practice Everywhere!

When you're doing anything, such as taking a shower, eating, dressing, or other activity, think, "I Dedicate the Merit of my activity for the benefit of all beings."

You can even transform sleep into the practice of virtue. If you go to sleep thinking "I will help to benefit all beings," your sleep will be transformative. You can also practice dream yoga to transform your dreams and practice lucid dreaming. Remember to do this before you go to sleep, even when you wake up during the night and then return to sleep.

Since we need to have a technique for accumulating merit in everyday life, even if we can't sit down and practice, if we can be present in the moment and think of others, we *are* practicing. In this way, every activity of life can become the practice of *bodhichitta*.

Six

An Introduction to Vajrayana: Medicine Buddha

ℬ ℬ ℬ ────────────────────────────────

Vajrayana Buddhism is a unique, important, and complex form of Buddhism that originated from Buddha Shakyamuni in India and spread throughout Tibet, Bhutan, Nepal, and Mongolia. It is the third major branch of Buddhism, along with Hinayana and Mahayana. Vajrayana Buddhism places special emphasis on the use of mantras and visualizations to attain enlightenment and liberation. It emphasizes the direct experience of these teachings.

The origins of Vajrayana can be traced back to India during the seventh century CE and developed by the great Indian Buddhist master Padmasambhava, also known as Guru Rinpoche. He is credited with the establishment and spread of the Vajrayana teachings from the Buddha throughout Tibet.

Vajrayana is a system designed for practitioners who have cultivated meditative experience. One of the unique features of Vajrayana is to accelerate the process of spiritual transformation. It is based on the understanding that the body, speech, and mind are interconnected and can be used to achieve our spiritual goals. This system uses a wide range of techniques, including visualization, mantra recitation, and making offerings to transform ordinary everyday experiences into spiritual practices.

Another important aspect of Vajrayana is the use of mandalas, which are intricate and colorful diagrams that represent the universe and the various deities and forces within it. Mandalas (such as sand mandalas) are used as tools for meditation and visualization.

Vajrayana Buddhism also places great importance and emphasis on the role of the teacher who is considered essential for transmitting the teachings and practices of the Vajrayana. The teacher is seen as a spiritual guide who helps the practitioner overcome obstacles on the path leading to enlightenment. The relationship between the teacher and the student is precious and is of utmost importance; they have a mutual bond. The student shows respect and devotion to the teacher by diligent practice, and the teacher, out of kindness and compassion, leads the student to discover his or her Buddha-nature.

The importance of Vajrayana Buddhism lies in its emphasis on the direct transmission of teachings from teacher to student in an unbroken lineage. Its focus is on inner transformation through its unique approach to meditation and visualization. The three defining features are:

1. *Direct Transmission.* As noted, the role of the teacher is considered essential. The teacher is seen as a source of direct transmission of teachings and practices conveyed through personal instruction and empowerment. This direct transmission is believed to be essential for the correct understanding and practice of Vajrayana Buddhism.

2. *Inner Transformation.* Through meditative practices, the importance of inner transformation is emphasized. These practices include the use of visualization and symbols intended to break down the dualistic perception of reality and lead to the realization of the non-dual nature of the mind.

3. *Meditation and Visualization.* These practices place great importance on meditation and are considered essential for cultivating the wisdom and compassion necessary for

enlightenment. In Vajrayana meditation, practitioners use visualization to transform their ordinary perception of reality into a sacred and pure perception of this world.

These methods reveal the true nature of reality and lead the practitioner to greater understanding and realization. The complex rituals and practices of Vajrayana Buddhism are intended to lead practitioners to a deeper understanding of the nature of their mind, Buddha-nature.

Introduction to Medicine Buddha

An example of this form of meditation is found in the following Medicine Buddha practice. His full name in Sanskrit is Bhaishajyaguru Vaiduryaprabha, the Medicine Buddha of Lapis Lazuli Light. He is called Sangye Menla in Tibetan.

Khenchen Thrangu Rinpoche gives us the setting for this particular sutra given in Vaisali, one of six major cities in India at the time of the Buddha. The Buddha gave an explanation about the Medicine Buddha, which would be known as "Sutra of the Medicine Buddha." It was the Bodhisattva Manjushri who made the request of the Buddha to turn the Wheel of Dharma. Before he begins his discourse, the Buddha enjoins Manjushri to "listen well, listen fully, and hold this in your mind." This has particular meaning with respect to how to listen to the Dharma teachings.

Rinpoche explains that the first injunction, "Listen well," means listen with appropriate motivation. If you have a good motivation for listening, then the Dharma you hear will be contained in a pure form in your mind. On the other hand, if you listen with an impure motivation with attachment or aversion, then your mind will become like a container or a cup that holds poison, and whatever is poured into it becomes tainted.

In the second injunction of the Buddha, "Listen fully," means listen attentively. You may have a good motivation for listening to the teachings, but if you are distracted, if you do not direct your mind to what is being said, then listening is of no use. Your mind will become like a cup turned upside down, and nothing can be poured into it.

And the third injunction is "Hold it in your mind." Even if you have good motivation and listen well, if you forget what is being taught, then it is lost from your mind. Your mind is then like a broken cup with holes in it; no matter how much is poured into it, it will all leak out again. So be diligent. "Listen well, listen fully, and hold these teachings in your mind." In other words, listen, contemplate, and practice these Dharma teachings to the best of your ability.

In these times of great stress, pain, and sickness, many rely on the Medicine Buddha meditation as a remedy for suffering of all kinds. The Buddha taught that the power of the mind is preeminent. The words medication and meditation are so similar because they come from the same Latin root word, *medeor*, meaning "to heal" or "to make whole." Whether we medicate or meditate, our goal is the same! Meditation is a healing activity.

During the writing of this book, the world was involved in a pandemic that took the lives of over 6.8 million people worldwide, with many more suffering from the aftermath of exposure to the virus, and the cultural and economic fallout also are still being experienced. However, many people did not get sick and were able to continue to stay healthy. I am happy to say I am one of those who never got sick with the virus. We practice Medicine Buddha meditation, not to replace medical treatment, but to enhance better health and healing outcomes. This practice purifies and helps remove the karmic causes of disease and creates the causes for health and well-being. As a result of this purification, we may see actual improvements in health problems.

Science does not contradict the profound power of the mind. On the contrary, numerous studies support the power of the mind, meditation, and mantra healing for everything, from migraines to depression, cognitive and mental health issues, and much more.

We know the great power of the mind and its healing capacity. The recent explosion of literature and science reports in professional journals has brought it to mainstream Western medicine. In addition, practical research has been going on in Asian countries such as, India, China, and Tibet for thousands of years by the great yogis of the past. This knowledge and wisdom have been passed down from the time of the Buddha to us.

The Medicine Buddha is a prominent figure in Mahayana and Vajrayana Buddhism and is revered for the ability to heal physical and mental ailments. The Medicine Buddha practice involves meditation, visualization, and recitation of mantras to invoke the blessings of the Medicine Buddha and receive this healing energy. Unsurprisingly, the Sanskrit word *mantra* means "mind protection."

The practice of Medicine Buddha is considered important for several reasons:

- *Healing.* The primary focus of the Medicine Buddha practice is to promote physical and mental health. By invoking the blessings of the Medicine Buddha, practitioners can experience healing themselves, as was my experience, and can also enhance the physical and mental healing of others.
- *Compassion.* The Medicine Buddha is considered a manifestation of the compassion of all Buddhas. By practicing the Medicine Buddha meditation, practitioners develop compassion and empathy toward others.
- *Wisdom.* The Medicine Buddha also is associated with the Perfection of Wisdom, which is considered a vital aspect of Buddhist practice. By meditating on the Medicine Buddha, practitioners develop wisdom and insight.

- **Protection.** The Medicine Buddha practice provides protection against the various forms of harm—physical, mental, emotional, and spiritual harm.
- **Transformation.** The practice of Medicine Buddha has the power to transform negative karma and lead to spiritual transformation and enlightenment.

This practice is a further application of *Shamatha* (calm-abiding) and *Vipashyana* (insight). When we meditate on the form of the Medicine Buddha and recite the mantra, we are practicing *Shamatha*. When we dissolve the visualization and the self into emptiness and realize we are meditating on the mere empty appearance that dissolves into emptiness, we are practicing *Vipashyana*. This purifies the mind of mental and emotional obscurations blocking the direct insight into the nature of our mind, our Buddha-nature.

The focal point of this healing practice is visualization. In the case of Medicine Buddha, for example, we visualize him as deep blue, the color of lapis lazuli. He wears the Dharma robes of a monk and is seated in the full cross-legged position on a lotus and moon disk throne. His right hand rests upon his knee with the palm facing outward in the mudra of granting blessings holding the stem of a myrobalan plant (*Terminalia chebula*), praised as the king among medicines because of its effectiveness in treating mental and physical diseases. And the left hand is resting on the lap, holding a begging bowl filled with medicinal nectar in the mudra representing meditative stability.

In the traditional Tibetan *thangka*, (elaborately painted wall hangings of various sizes that display different images of Buddhist iconography), Medicine Buddha is often shown in the company of seven other Medicine Buddha brothers that surround him; one of whom is Shakyamuni Buddha. The *thangka* further depicts the eastern Buddha realm known as the Pure Land of Lapis Lazuli, Palace of Beauty.

The most distinctive feature of the Medicine Buddha is his deep blue lapis lazuli color. The stone lapis lazuli has been prized by Asian and European cultures for more than six thousand years. Traditionally, this stone was used to symbolize that which is pure or rare. It is said to have strengthening qualities for those who wear it, along with medicinal benefits to boost immunity, lower blood pressure, reduce inflammation, relieve insomnia, depression, and benefit the nervous and respiratory systems. It is associated with strength and courage, royalty and wisdom, intellect and truth.

Additionally, the Medicine Buddha is revered as the source of all healing arts and "patron saint" for all physicians! It is through these teachings that the four medical tantras comprise the basis of Traditional Tibetan Medicine (TTM). According to the four tantras, the fundamental cause of every disease is the three poisons of anger, desire, and ignorance. These three poisons lead to imbalances in the elements that lead to disturbances in the three humors. Humors maintain and nourish the different systems of the body, through the balance of phlegm (earth and water elements), wind (air element), and bile (fire element) constitutional types.

Treatment of disease and maintenance of health is a matter of bringing the elements of the body, including, earth, water, fire, and air, into proper balance. This is accomplished through four progressive types of treatments. The first involves assessing the person's diet. The second involves the person's behavior and daily activities and making lifestyle changes. The third intervention, if these first two prove ineffective, is to prescribe medicine in the form of herbs or other substances. If this should fail, we can resort to stronger, more direct, external forms of therapy, such as massage, cupping, acupuncture, and moxibustion.

However, these are types of treatments that will not have lasting effects unless they are accompanied by spiritual transformation. If ignorance and delusions remain fixed, they will give rise to disease and recurring suffering in samsara. The Medicine Buddha is referred to as the Supreme Physician, not only because of his great ability to heal disease, but also because of the cultivation of great compassion, wisdom, and skill to diagnose and treat the root cause underlying all mental and physical disease.

NAMO BEKANDZE MAHA RADZAYE

Homage to the Great King of Medicine

Prayer to Medicine Buddha

I beseech you, blessed Medicine Buddha,
Who's sky-colored, brilliant body of lapis lazuli
Signifies omniscient wisdom and compassion
As vast and limitless as space,
Please grant your blessings.

I beseech you, blessed Medicine Buddha,
Holding in your right hand the king of medicines
Symbolizing your vow to help all beings
Plagued by many diseases,
Please grant your blessings.

I beseech you blessed Medicine Buddha,
The left hand holds a bowl of nectar
Symbolizing your vow to give the glorious,
Undying nectar of the Dharma
Which transcends the degenerations of old age,
Sickness and death,
Please grant your blessings.

You may find chanting the mantra of Medicine Buddha soothing, relaxing, and healing. It is another skillful means taught to tame our mind used in conjunction with our sitting practice. The Medicine Buddha mantra can be chanted in Sanskrit or Tibetan. Below is the Tibetan and Sanskrit transliteration of the Medicine Buddha mantra:

Mantra: *Tayata Om Bekandze Bekandze Maha Bekandze Radza Samudgate Soha.*

Pronounced: Tay-ah-tah, Om, beck-and-zay beck-and-zay, ma-ha beck-and-zay, rad-zuh sum-ood-gut-eh, so-ha.

Sanskrit: Tadyatha Om Bhaisajye Bhaisajye Mahabhaisajye Raja Samudgate Svaha.

The Medicine Buddha mantra is a powerful tool in Mahayana and Vajrayana Buddhism for invoking the blessings of the Medicine Buddha, promoting healing, and cultivating wisdom and compassion. It is even written in the Sutras that if you speak the name of the Medicine Buddha in the ears of a dying human or animal, they will be insured good rebirth, regardless of past karma, and be spared from the lower realms.

The source for this presentation was compiled and written from the teachings on Medicine Buddha practice by our kind teachers Khenpo Karthar Rinpoche and Khenchen Thrangu Rinpoche. It was Khenpo Rinpoche who gave me the reading transmission, the "*lung*," and said it would be good to teach it. With that in mind, the Short Medicine Buddha practice is presented below. In addition, and highly recommended, is a wonderful book titled *Medicine Buddha Teaching*, by Khenchen Thrangu Rinpoche. It shares the complete teaching and is listed in the *Bibliography and Recommended-Reading* section of this book.

A Short Practice of Medicine Buddha

1. Preliminaries

What you need to begin:

- Find a quiet place for the next twenty minutes, prepare a straight-backed chair or meditation cushion, and take your seat.
- Have a *mala*, Buddhist prayer beads with 108 beads, available to count mantras. Mala beads are the traditional way of keeping track

of your mantra count. A wrist mala typically has twenty-seven beads, and the standard *mala* has 108 beads (*see Appendix E for more on the use of a mala*).

- Your shrine room should be clean and comfortable with a little table for your text, a flower, or incense. Having a statue or picture of Medicine Buddha in front of you is good to help with visualization. Add whatever else you would like to create a sacred space for practice that makes you happy. Keep it simple.

2. Meditation

Calm the mind with a few minutes of Shamatha sitting meditation.

Visualize yourself as Medicine Buddha, sitting on a lotus and moon disk seat. Next, imagine that in front and slightly above you is another Medicine Buddha, seated on a beautiful lotus throne in the center of a brilliant moon disk.

His body is a dark blue and is the nature of light, like a rainbow or a hologram, vivid but intangible. He gazes at you with love, like a mother for her only child.

Surrounding the Medicine Buddha in front of you are his retinue of seven other Medicine Buddhas, as well as countless other Buddhas and Bodhisattvas.

Everything you visualize should be seen as non-solid and made of light, like a rainbow in the sky. Most importantly, have confidence that he is actually there with you. Try to cultivate that feeling of the presence of Medicine Buddha.

Figure 3: Medicine Buddha

3. In the Presence of Medicine Buddha

In the presence of the Medicine Buddha, request the help needed, for example, to quell worry, fear and insecurity, sickness or pain, and physical, mental, or emotional distress. Have total confidence in the Medicine Buddha's power to help.

Visualize the Medicine Buddha receiving your request and responding to it. Instantly, deep, blue-colored healing light, syllables from his mantra, small Medicine Buddha images, and his begging bowl filled with nectar and with his blessings all flow into you and fill your body with love and vitality.

From Medicine Buddha's heart comes healing rays of light that enter, filling your body (or the being for whom you are practicing) with healing light, bringing peace of mind and healing where needed. You can direct the healing lights and nectars to any specific parts of the body.

4. Refuge and Bodhichitta Prayer

Then, recite the Refuge and Bodhichitta Prayer (transliteration of the Tibetan and translation) as follows:

Refuge and Bodhichitta Prayer

HUNG KUN DOK BEN DUR YA YI RI WO DRA

Hung. Your body is the color of a mountain of lapis lazuli,

DRO WA SEM CHEN NAY CHI DU NGAL SEL

You dispel the suffering of disease from all sentient beings.

CHANG CHUB SEM PA JAY CHI KOR JI KOR

Your retinue of seven other Medicine Buddhas
and eight Bodhisattvas surrounds you.

RIN CHEN MEN DZIN LHA LA CHA TSAL TO

I praise and pay homage to the deity who holds the precious medicine.

(Repeat three times.)

Taking refuge ensures that your practice follows the correct path of Dharma; cultivating the Bodhisattva attitude (wishing to gain enlightenment to benefit others) ensures that your practice will not be limited and will be vast in its ability to benefit others.

5. Medicine Buddha Mantra and Visualization

Next, recite the Medicine Buddha mantra at least 108 times (see pronunciation above).

TAYATA OM BEKENDZE BEKENDZE MAHABEKENDZE
RADZA SAMUDGATE SOHA

The Medicine Buddha mantra is chanted with the intention of invoking the healing power and blessing of the Medicine Buddha to alleviate suffering, promote physical and mental well-being, and attain enlightenment. Reciting this mantra can bring about healing, peace of mind, and spiritual awakening.

Figure 4: Medicine Buddha Radiating Healing Light

While you are reciting the mantra, visualize the following: in your heart as the Medicine Buddha is a flat moon disk and a HUNG, the seed syllable of the Medicine Buddha. You can also visualize the Tibetan syllable (*see the Tibetan letter HUNG on the inside title page*) surrounded by the syllables of the Medicine Buddha mantra.

If you have trouble visualizing the syllables, you can see the seed syllable as lapis lazuli-colored light and the mantra as a circle of lapis lazuli beads of light surrounding the syllable HUNG.

Imagine that many light rays come from the mantra and seed syllable HUNG in your heart and travel out to the Medicine Buddha in front of you. These light rays touch his heart, awakening his compassion.

Then, from the heart of the Medicine Buddha in front of you, light rays travel out to the Eastern realm of the actual Medicine Buddha. The light rays make offerings to the Medicine Buddha and his retinue of awakened beings. These offerings awaken their compassion and remind them of their promises and aspirations to benefit all beings.

The actual Medicine Buddha sends blessings down from his heavenly realm, and they shower you like snowflakes of blessings that dissolve into you and the visualized Medicine Buddha in front of you.

The blessing of the Medicine Buddha's body comes in the form of small images of the Medicine Buddha.

The blessings of the Medicine Buddha's speech come in the form of strings of his mantra.

The blessing of the Medicine Buddha's mind comes in the form of his begging bowl filled with the nectar of wisdom and healing, and the arura (myrobalan) fruit held in the Medicine Buddha's right hand.

Think that as you receive these blessings, they wash away all your negative karma, all your illness, and all your ignorance and confusion. Think then that the blessings give you peace, health, happiness, contentment, and all the qualities you feel you need, such as courage, wisdom, compassion, or patience.

If you are doing this practice for another person, see the blessings raining down on that person.

After you have finished the visualization and mantra recitation, rest in the lucid clarity of your Buddha-nature.

Dedicate the Merit as shown in the *Dedicating the Merit* Section 7 below.

6. Medicine Buddha Alternate Visualization

If the above steps are too difficult, then you can do the following simple alternate visualization:

Visualize a small form of the Medicine Buddha, about four inches high, in the part of your body or the body of another person injured or afflicted with illness.

As you recite the mantra, imagine that this form of the Medicine Buddha gives off the blue light and nectar of healing and wisdom. This eliminates illness and gives health, happiness, and well-being in body, mind, and spirit.

The Medicine Buddha mantra is recited 108 times along with the visualization.

TAYATA OM BEKENDZE BEKENDZE MAHABEKENDZE
RADZA SAMUDGATE SOHA

Visualize dissolving the Medicine Buddha and nectars image into you,
into the Hung in your heart into emptiness. All is emptiness.

As with the standard mantra and visualization above, Dedicate the
Merit as shown in the next section.

7. Dedication of Merit

Now it is time to Dedicate the Merit by chanting the following:

SEM CHEN NAY PA JI NYAY PA.
May the many sentient beings who are sick,

NYUR TU NAY LAY TAR JUR CHIK
Quickly be freed from sickness.

DRO WAY NAY NI MA LU PA
And may all the sicknesses of beings

TAK TU JUNG WA MAY PAR SHOK
Never arise again.

We pray that all beings be freed from illness and
confusion and quickly attain Buddhahood.

8. Concluding Prayer for All Medicine Buddha Practices

Say aloud or silently the following Medicine Buddha prayer:

Medicine Buddha, who is compassionate equally to all beings, the very hearing of whose name pacifies the three lower realms. Medicine Buddha, who eliminates the illnesses of the three poisons, may there be the goodness of the lapis lazuli light.

May sentient beings, whatever illnesses they suffer, be liberated quickly from those illnesses. May all the illnesses of beings, without exception, never arise again.

May medicines be effective and may the intentions of the recitation of the secret mantra path be accomplished. May all beings attain a compassionate mind.

This completes the short healing Medicine Buddha practice.

Concluding Thoughts

All the above-mentioned practices have profound healing potential. In fact, meditation has been shown to have a very positive impact on the mind and body. The Harvard Medical School cardiologist, Dr. Herbert Benson, author of *The Relaxation Response*, whose research I used in my doctoral dissertation, went on to investigate how to help his patients heal themselves. He studied different methods of meditation and tested to see which were best suited for self-healing.

He found it particularly striking that not only is self-repair boosted, but also immune system function is enhanced by endorphin production, and serotonin levels are enhanced for better regulation of mood, appetite, sleep, and overall well-being. It was found that over time the benefits continued to increase. He continued his research and wrote a second book, *Beyond the Relaxation Response*, after traveling to Tibet and studying the Yogis in the Himalayan region.

Recent studies show how meditation can help manage chronic inflammatory conditions, such as arthritis, asthma, and inflammatory bowel syndrome (IBS), to name a few. It has even been shown to slow the rate of aging by elevating levels of telomerase, the enzyme supporting the resilience of the telomeres that cap our DNA and extend life.

However, the recent discoveries in brain science disclose even more benefits of meditation. Our brains have the amazing ability to change themselves! This is called neuroplasticity. Our brains are not fixed structures but are dynamic systems that are constantly changing and evolving in response to the environment. This research has shown that the brain is more malleable and responsive than previously imagined. It is now known that neuroplasticity also has important implications for understanding the relationship between the mind and body.

One of the primary features of neuroplasticity is that it is activity-dependent, which means the changes in the brain are driven by experiences and activities. For example, if a person engages in a particular activity repeatedly, such as meditation, the brain will adapt to these experiences and develop new neural connections that support these activities, changing the brain and our mind. These findings have also found their way into the emerging science called psychoneuroimmunology (PNI), an interdisciplinary field that studies the relationship between psychological processes, the nervous system, and the immune system. The research in PNI has demonstrated the positive effects of meditation on immune function and overall physical and mental health.

Because of this capacity, we can radically change our thought patterns to have a more loving and compassionate experience. With these practices, we come to rest in the natural clarity of the mind, ultimately revealing the very nature of who we are with the direct experience of our own Buddha-nature. This is the answer to the question we initially asked, "Who am I?" With this understanding and with the highest motivation, in the spirit of the Bodhisattvas, we wish to attain Buddhahood for the benefit of all beings.

To briefly review, the essence of Buddhist teachings is the Four Noble Truths and following the Noble Eightfold Path. These are considered the foundation of Buddhism and provide a framework for understanding the nature of suffering and showing the path to liberation from it. So please do your best to remember:

The Four Noble Truths:

The Truth of Suffering: all beings experience suffering, physical or mental.

The Truth of the Cause of Suffering: attachment, craving, and ignorance.

The Truth of the Cessation of Suffering: it is possible to end suffering by letting go of attachment and craving.

The Truth of the Path Leading to the Cessation of Suffering: The Noble Eightfold Path leads to the cessation of suffering.

The Noble Eightfold Path:

Right View: understanding the Four Noble Truths and the nature of reality.

Right Thought: cultivating wholesome intentions, such as compassion and generosity.

Right Speech: speaking truthfully and kindly.

Right Action: acting ethically and in accordance with the precepts.

Right Livelihood: earning a living in a way that is ethical and does not cause harm.

Right Effort: cultivating wholesome qualities and letting go of unwholesome ones.

Right Mindfulness: developing increasing awareness of the present moment, remaining at ease and without distraction. Shamatha meditation is training to make the mind stable.

Right Meditation: having developed our capacity to rest the mind in meditative absorption, we are able to directly experience the nature of our mind, our Buddha-nature.

To accomplish the goal of these teachings, we must begin cultivating all factors of the Noble Eightfold Path. This involves developing the correct view, wisdom, ethical conduct, and mental discipline through meditation, mindfulness, and compassionate action. By doing so, we can gradually overcome attachment, ego-clinging, and craving.

In following the Hinayana path and cultivating samadhi through Shamatha and Vipashyana, we can tame our mind and experience the cessation of suffering. We also can realize our natural, ever-present, clear, and lucid Awakened Mind and attain the bliss of Nirvana.

However, we still must cultivate Bodhichitta, the mind of enlightenment. In the Mahayana, the "greater vehicle," we are not just concerned for ourselves, but feel compassion for *all* suffering beings. We cultivate the Bodhisattva attitude. We cultivate the two wings of the bird, wisdom and compassion, as requisites for achieving the goal of Buddhahood. We also cultivate an unbiased love and compassion and the wish to free all beings from the suffering of samsara. To assist doing so, please remember the Four Immeasurables, Tonglen, and the Six Perfections!

Earlier in the text I mentioned the key differences between the sutra approach and the Vajrayana approach. The *sutra* approach takes longer and is sometimes called "the analytical approach." Through this analysis, we conclude that the mind's essence is empty, has a lucid clarity, and Buddha-nature exists in all beings. However, this is realized primarily through a process of logical deduction.

In the *Vajrayana* path, Vipashyana takes on a different meaning. Vipashyana, translated into Tibetan is *lhaktong*. *Tong* means "to see" and *lhak* means "superior." We can see it as the direct attainment of superior transcendent insight. This direct insight is not inferential or deductive; it is the direct experience of our Buddha-nature. This meditative absorption in the direct experience of our mind's Buddha-nature leads to the full awakening of a Buddha.

We have just gently scratched the surface of the Buddha's teaching. The Buddha taught 84,000 different aspects of practice, and it would be impossible to master all of these. Fortunately, we don't have to master all of them to attain Buddhahood. In fact, just sincerely entering the path and diligently practicing one of these methods eventually will lead to perfect enlightenment.

We have been on this journey since beginningless time! Right here, right now, we have the exquisite good fortune to have been born human, with all the qualities and conditions needed to make this precious human birth meaningful. So let us take advantage of this opportunity and use these blessings wisely.

I hope you will continue to study and practice what you have learned and apply it in your daily life for your benefit and for the benefit of all beings and their ultimate enlightenment. We *can* tame this monkey mind and realize the essence of the truth taught by the Buddha.

May you benefit from this reading (or listening) and feel inspired to continue on the path to freedom. May you be released from the chains of attachment, anger, and wrong views. May you come to know who you truly are. May all be auspicious for you!

The Appendices

Appendix A

The Three-Year Retreat Experience

The subject of meditation and a three-year, three-month retreat can seem mysterious and very foreign to the Western mind. We really don't have any equivalent in our culture. However, in our lineage, retreat is one of the most important practices of Vajrayana Buddhism. Within the four main monastic schools previously mentioned, it is only the Nyingma and Kagyu that grant the title Lama to those who have completed such retreats. This brief account is intended to give a demystified description of this training.

The word "Lama" refers to a qualified teacher capable of guiding a student through the stages of spiritual development. In the Buddhist tradition of training, study, and practice, find their fruition in meditation. Study and meditation are practiced together. However, there are different paths. Scholars of various traditions are more attracted to monastic colleges and study the texts and commentaries, while those who wish to train directly under the tutelage of a meditation master enter retreats designed to impart a thorough training in meditation.

The meditation retreat centers are small, self-sufficient communities that stand apart from a larger affiliated monastery. For example, my retreat at Karme Ling is an isolated and secluded location in Delhi, New York, which is in the beautiful Catskill Mountains and is about a 90-minute drive from Karma Triyana Dharmachakra in Woodstock.

From the outside, the retreat center looks like a fortress. It has a high wooden fence all around it and a large, gated entrance. Retreatants cannot see over the fence, and outsiders can't see inside. This adds to the feeling of leaving the world behind. Those entering retreat do leave behind possessions, duties, and responsibilities and fully devote themselves to the practice of Buddhadharma. No one other than those directly involved with the retreat activities are allowed in for the duration of the retreat. Only the cook, retreat manager, and teachers are permitted to enter.

At age fifty, I entered retreat to realize the truth the Buddha taught. Although I had been practicing for decades prior to the retreat, I still felt like a novice as much of this was new to me.

I didn't start retreat at Karme Ling until after a brief stay at Karma Triyana Dharmachakra Monastery where I began the pre-retreat training. We immediately began activities starting with all the various empowerments given by Khenchen Thrangu Rinpoche needed for the many pujas done during the retreat.

We learned to make many kinds of *torma* (food offerings usually made from oatmeal, butter and oil) and *gyens* (decoration that go on the *tormas* usually made with butter) used as offerings in all daily pujas. Much of the time between practice sessions is used to make tormas for group and personal use. We also learned to play all the different musical instruments used in daily practice: *damaru*, (a small hand drum), bells, cymbals, large ceremonial drum, *gyaling*, (a double reed woodwind instrument), *kangling* (a thigh bone trumpet used in Chod practice), and *radung* (a large ceremonial horn.)

Our teachers were patient and committed to their job in making us proficient in the various skills needed in the retreat. All of this was new to me and a bit daunting. After the first two months of pre-retreat, the experience already was life-changing! I realized at a deeper level that I was about to enter another world, one I was not accustomed to, including sleeping in a 'meditation box' designed for this purpose. More about that later.

Retreat is the hallmark of the Karma Kagyu lineage and has been practiced for centuries. The tradition originated from the Buddha and is found in the teachings of the Kalachakra tantra (See Bibliography, Jamgon Kongtrul, *Treasury of Knowledge, Book One: Myriad Worlds*). The practice of retreat was made popular by the great Rimé masters, Jamgon Kongtrul and Jamyang Khyentse Wangpo. It is an intense, systematic training in advanced meditation techniques that takes place at an isolated location. A group of practitioners take the retreat together under a qualified teacher, and during this period, the only contact is with fellow retreatants. One does not leave the retreat grounds or interact with anyone else—no phones, computers, newspapers, or contact with the outside world.

Khenpo Rinpoche was able to bring this retreat facility to fruition as envisioned by the Sixteenth Karmapa. He supervised the construction of two retreat buildings: one for women retreatants to live and practice and one for men. A third building, the Lama House, was constructed for visiting Rinpoches and guests. On January 23, 1993, the first retreat at Karme Ling began and has continued up until now. Rinpoche's explanations of these meditations and practices, along with excellent translations from Tibetan to English, are regarded as the finest in the Karma Kagyu lineage. I entered the third retreat in January 2000.

There is also the Dewachen Columbarium on the grounds of the Karme Ling property separate from the retreat center. This is where the ashes of the deceased are housed in urns and placed in special recesses in the wall and regularly prayed for. It is where my ashes will be placed after my death. Lamps may be requested and offered in the Columbarium Lamp House at any time for the deceased and for the health of living beings, for blessings during times of trouble, or for any other personal reasons. Offering lamps is an excellent method for accumulating merit, purifying illness, and dispelling obstacles for yourself and your loved ones.

Anyone wishing to begin the traditional three-year retreat must first get permission from the retreat master; for me, that was the venerable Khenpo Karthar Rinpoche. All the retreat practices are done in Tibetan; thus, all retreatants are required to be able to read Tibetan before beginning the retreat. The final requirement is to have completed the four foundations of *ngondro*.

The retreat begins every four years on the twenty-second day of the ninth lunar month in the Tibetan calendar, the auspicious day of the Lhabab Duchen. This is one of the four great observances for Buddhist practitioners and a very auspicious day to begin. For convenience, we usually say it lasts for three years and three months. It is actually three years and three fortnights (a fortnight is two weeks).

The practices currently done in retreat are:

- Ngondro (four months).
- Mahamudra (one month).
- Karma Pakshi (one month).
- White Tara (one month).
- Guru Yoga (three months) of one of the following: Marpa, Milarepa, or Gampopa.
- Vajrayogini (nine months).
- Six Yogas of Naropa (seven months).
- Chakrasamvara (seven months).
- Amitabha (two months).
- Gyalwa Gyamtso (six months).

In our retreat, in addition to Rinpoche, there were seven men, including myself, as well as our cook and the retreat manager. I won't go into the specific details of our day-to-day practice, but we followed a similar daily schedule. A typical day in the retreat would begin at 4:00 a.m. and end at 9:00 p.m., seven days a week: no vacation, holidays, or time-off. Retreatants do not leave their rooms during practice sessions, except to go to the bathroom. Retreatants are expected to remain in silence, except for the necessary talking during meal breaks about retreat matters and asking Rinpoche practice questions. This was not strictly enforced, and we could converse at mealtimes. We also could continue to maintain silence. Maintaining mindfulness is the key point.

Each retreatant has their own room where they spend most of the day in formal meditation practice. In our retreat everything was housed in one building. Within that building there was a large shrine room for teachings and group practices held twice daily, a room for yoga practice (Trulkor), kitchen, dining room, and communal showers and toilets. There was an identical building for the women's retreat that was a short distance away and out of sight from the men's retreat house.

Our individual rooms had just enough space for a small shrine, a small bookcase, and enough floor space to stretch out when doing full prostrations for the ngondro practice. Rooms also had a window that opened onto the courtyard. Because of the high wooden fence that surrounded the building, we could only see the sky and the tops of the trees. This proved to be another reminder of impermanence. I observed the gradual change of the seasons by the transformation of the leaves on the Maple trees and the migration of the birds throughout the year. The birds, especially the migrating Sandhill Cranes with their loud, shrill call flying in formation overhead announced the seasonal changes and became my friends as viewed from my window. I was familiar with their migration because historically, they would come to Florida for the winter arriving around Thanksgiving and leave to fly back to Canada around Valentine's Day for the summer!

Each room also was furnished with a "meditation box." This served as both our meditation seat and bed. (See picture below.) The "box" is considered ideal for meditative body alignment. We learned how to sleep in this seated, upright position as part of our retreat practice. This has special significance for the practices, such as Dream Yoga, one of the Six Yogas of Naropa.

One remains in their meditation box during practice sessions and at night when sleeping. It is an open, wooden box that has three low sides and a high back to rest against. Its base and back structure is about 36-by-36-inches, and its sides are 18 inches tall. It has a horizontal board that slides toward and away from your torso as needed, for it functions like a table upon which study materials and offerings are placed.

Figure 5: Vajrayana Buddhism Retreat's Meditation Box

Residents in retreat are also provided with a set of monk's robes that are worn throughout the retreat and we behave like the ordained sangha. The same is true for the women. This is done to remove any attachments to clothes that are often associated as symbols of status and position. Everyone is treated equally, regardless of their wealth, position and social status that may have existed prior to entering retreat.

As for the meals, the men's and women's houses have their own cooks who prepare breakfast and lunch. Retreatants can prepare whatever evening meal they would like from leftovers or from the simple foods provided, using a hot plate, toaster, microwave, and the refrigerator outside the main kitchen for this purpose. Food is strictly vegetarian with vegan options.

The cook does all the shopping for the retreatants' food and personal needs during the retreat.

When one begins, there is a commitment to complete the retreat. Leaving constitutes breaking *samaya*, the vow that binds the practitioner to their practice and to their teacher, and if broken, it is considered to have serious karmic consequences. Although retreatants are not allowed to leave the retreat grounds, exceptions are made in the case of serious illness.

It was a very profound and challenging endeavor. Obstacles came up during this time that challenged me. This is not at all unusual. Many who have undergone this rigorous training have experienced the upsurge of physical, mental, and emotional challenges that bubble up from the depths of our being. That is 'grist for the mill' and where the practice of meditation is so valuable. Letting go of my old structures and beliefs was not easy and was accompanied by some degree of suffering that I considered growing pains. Fortunately, there is good news: with increasing insight comes less suffering. It is about taming the mind – and I did indeed learn to tame my mind!

I am very grateful for the teachings and practices done in the retreat. Putting these teachings into practice in such an intense way was a powerful catalyst for change. This change I readily accepted! Far from seeing the experience ending in enlightenment, I see it as a firm foundation on which to build an ongoing practice in everyday life.

With joyful perseverance, I did complete the retreat in March 2003. The significance, power, and influence this training had on me changed the direction of my life. Briefly stated, these intensive practices done daily over three years and three months were transformative. I feel very fortunate and grateful to have had the opportunity for training, study, and practice under the supervision and guidance of Khenpo Karthar Rinpoche that this retreat provided.

APPENDIX B

Tibetan Buddhism and Our Mahamudra Lineage

What is *Mahamudra*? Mahamudra meditation originated in the Mahayana and Vajrayana traditions of Buddhism. It is a practice that aims to help practitioners achieve a state of perfect enlightenment or realization of the ultimate nature of mind, Buddha-nature. The word Mahamudra is derived from Sanskrit and could be translated as "great seal" or "great symbol." It is a term used to describe the ultimate nature of reality, beyond concepts and words.

In Mahamudra meditation, practitioners focus on the direct realization of the nature of mind to attain the perfect Awakened Mind. This is done through the practice of Shamatha (tranquility) and Vipashyana (insight), leading to Mahamudra. One of the key aspects of Mahamudra meditation is the recognition of the nature of the mind as being essentially pure and unchanging, regardless of the content of one's thoughts or experiences. This recognition leads to a profound sense of inner peace and freedom from suffering.

Mahamudra meditation is traditionally taught by a qualified teacher, and it is often practiced in conjunction with other forms of Buddhist practice, such as the cultivation of ethics, compassion, and wisdom. It is considered an advanced practice and typically is only taught to experienced practitioners who have already established a strong foundation in the basics of Buddhist meditation.

Here are some of the key aspects of Mahamudra meditation and its importance:

- *Direct Realization.* Mahamudra meditation is a direct path to realizing the ultimate nature of the mind. It involves looking directly into the nature of the mind, without conceptual elaboration or analysis, and experiencing the true nature of reality as it is, unelaborated and uncontrived.
- *Non-dual Awareness.* Mahamudra meditation emphasizes the non-dual nature of awareness, which is considered the ultimate reality. By meditating on the nature of the mind, practitioners can develop a direct experience of non-duality and overcome the dualistic perception of self and others.
- *Integration of Practice and Daily Life.* Mahamudra meditation is not just a formal practice, but also a way of life. Practitioners are encouraged to integrate their meditation practice with their daily activities. The Buddha said to cultivate mindfulness and awareness in all aspects of our lives, sitting, standing, walking, and lying down. Everything becomes enlightened activity as we become more mindful.
- *Teacher-Student Relationship.* In Mahamudra practice, the relationship between the teacher and the student is considered very special. The teacher is seen as the source of guidance, inspiration, and blessing. The student carefully follows the instructions of the teacher with devotion and sincerity.

Mahamudra is considered the quintessential practice of the Kagyu tradition. It is the direct path to realizing the ultimate nature of reality and the attainment of Awakening. The emphasis on non-dual awareness, integration of practice in daily life, and the importance of the teacher-student relationship makes it a powerful tool for spiritual transformation.

Here is a brief history of our Mahamudra lineage that will shed some light on the importance of a lineage directly from teacher to student.

The four principal schools of Tibetan Buddhism are Nyingma, Kagyu, Gelug, and Sakya. The Kagyu school traces its lineage from the primordial Buddha Vajradhara to the Indian Mahasiddhas Tilopa and to his student Naropa. The stories about the lives of the great lineage masters are remarkable and inspirational.

Other masters of the lineage include Marpa, a Tibetan who made the difficult journey from Tibet to India three times to bring the teachings of the Buddha to Tibet. His student, the great Tibetan yogi Milarepa, passed them down to his student Gampopa, and he to his student, the First Karmapa, Dusum Khyenpa. Each of them was a master who was taught by their teachers and continued our Mahamudra lineage to the current 17th Gyalwang Karmapa, Ogyen Trinley Dorje (See Bibliography, Khenchen Thrangu Rinpoche, *The Mahamudra Lineage Prayer*).

We have celebrated over 900 years of the Kagyu tradition. Beings identified as reincarnations of the previous master are known as *Tulkus*. There have been many recognized Tulkus in the Tibetan Buddhist tradition. The First Karmapa, Dusum Khyenpa, was the first Tulku of the seventeen incarnations who would follow to be recognized as *Karmapa*. The 16th Gyalwa Karmapa, Rangjung Rigpe Dorje, a Tibetan, was one of the first to come to the United States to disseminate the teachings of the Buddha to Westerners. He sent many teachers to the West to teach the Dharma. One of those was my teacher, Khenpo Karthar Rinpoche.

The 16th Karmapa passed away, *parinirvana*, in Chicago in 1981. The current *Karmapa* was discovered several years later, a child from a nomadic family in Tibet. The 16th Karmapa, like his predecessors, had left a letter before he died with another master of our lineage, Tai Situ Rinpoche. This letter described and named the place of his next birth, where he could be found, the name of his parents, and other details to allow the search party to find and identify him. The 14th Dalai Lama also confirmed this in a prophetic dream he had. This was the case with each of the seventeen Karmapas, including our present 17th Karmapa, Ogyen Trinley Dorje. He is said to be destined to become the 6th Buddha of this fortunate eon. Reading about the lives of these realized masters is inspirational and highly recommended.

Khenpo Rinpoche was born in 1924 in Eastern Tibet and received much of his training at Thrangu Monastery. Because of the Communist invasion in 1958, Rinpoche was forced to leave Tibet and fled as a refugee to India. It was a dangerous and difficult journey. Lacking food and other supplies and dodging bullets, they did arrive safely in India. But conditions were not good there. Many people became ill. Rinpoche was one of those. It took him a long time to recover.

In 1967, he was requested to teach the monks at Rumtek Monastery in Sikkim, the seat in exile of the 16th Gyalwa Karmapa. In 1975, he received the title of Choje Lama (Supreme Dharma Master). That next spring, he left Sikkim and Rumtek Monastery to go to the United States as requested by the Gyalwa Karmapa. He and a small group of monks arrived in New York City and began teaching around New York and beyond. This began the early development of the Karma Kagyu lineage in the United States.

I received my initial Refuge Vows from Khenpo Rinpoche, and as a result of his kindness and compassion, I was able to complete the three-year retreat and later travel with him to China, India, Nepal, and Tibet to receive teachings and the Gelong vows of a Bhikshu from Khenchen Thrangu Rinpoche, and the Bodhisattva Vow from Ogyen Trinley Dorje, the 17th Gyalwa Karmapa.

Khenpo Rinpoche has been the quintessential role model of how to be a compassionate guide to suffering beings. He served as abbot of Karma Triyana Dharmachakra (KTD) Monastery since its opening on the auspicious day of Saga Dawa, May 25, 1978, in Woodstock, New York, as the 16th Gyalwa Karmapa had requested. He also served as the spiritual guide to more than thirty-five satellite centers in the United States and around the world. In addition, he supervised the building of the Karme Ling Retreat Center and was the retreat master. He completed all the wishes of his teacher, the 16th Karmapa, working compassionately for the benefit of all beings.

Another esteemed teacher I wish to acknowledge is Khenchen Thrangu Rinpoche (1933–2023), who was my ordination master and bestowed the Getsul (intermediate) vows and Gelong (complete) vows of full ordination of a Bhikshu (monk) at Namo Buddha Monastery in Nepal. He was the tutor of the 17th Karmapa and is considered one of the foremost Tibetan Buddhist masters in our Karma Kagyu lineage. His passing into parinirvana was on the auspicious day of Saga Dawa, June 4, 2023.

Appendix C

Lama Losang's Story: My Precious Teacher Khenpo Karthar Rinpoche — Interview Transcript

Figure 6: Khenpo Karthar Rinpoche and Lama Losang

From an interview by Lama Karma Sonam with Lama Losang, celebrating the life of Khenpo Karthar Rinpoche shortly after his parinirvana at the age of ninety-six, on October 6, 2019.

Interviewer: Tell us about yourself and how you met Khenpo Rinpoche.

My name is Lama Losang (David Bole). I live in Gainesville, Florida, and am currently the spiritual director for the KTC centers in Florida. Here is a brief introduction to the circumstances of how I first met Rinpoche. It all began when I was attending the University of Florida. I took a psychology course and met my professor, Sidney Jourard, who was teaching a new field of study called transpersonal psychology. In class and in my reading, there were many references to Buddhism and the teachings of the Buddha. These teachings immediately resonated with me. Training the mind to achieve enlightenment made perfect sense to me. I saw Buddhism as a supreme psychology.

Along with two other students of Khenpo Rinpoche, Francis and her husband Joe Norwood, we began a Buddhist reading and study group in Gainesville. Because of Francis's previous connection, we invited Khenpo Rinpoche to come for a weekend teaching. When I saw his demeanor, heard his teaching, and witnessed how he engaged people with such loving-kindness and concern, I thought now here is a teacher that I can put my trust in. I have been his student since that time. That was in 1986!

It is very important for people to find the truth. And that is really what the Buddha taught. It is mind-training that can lead to lasting happiness. It's about finding the truth in your heart and practicing that truth in your everyday life. There are some very good role models, although they are hard to find. Khenpo Karthar Rinpoche is one of those role models that I've had the good fortune to know and to study with. He has certainly made an indelible impression on me.

There is one event that still remains with me from our first meeting almost four decades ago. When Rinpoche arrived in Gainesville for his teaching, we picked him up at the airport. My wife Joy and I had the honor and privilege to have him stay with us at our house for the duration of his stay.

The next day, after breakfast, Rinpoche wanted to take a bath. Joy prepared his bath and got everything ready. Rinpoche went in, and shortly afterward, we heard him call out. We went to check and saw Rinpoche standing outside the bathtub with a towel around him. He was pointing in the tub at a little green tree frog that had jumped into the bath water. It was clear that Rinpoche was concerned, not about himself, but for the little frog. We quickly got the frog out of the water, and Rinpoche chanted a mantra and gave his blessing. When Rinpoche saw the little green tree frog was okay, we released it back into the garden, and it hopped away. The concern and care Rinpoche showed toward that little frog deeply impressed me. It seemed as if the little creature was like his own child. This was an example of his caring and love that he showed for all living beings.

That weekend we had a great teaching—an introduction to Tibetan Buddhism. We all felt grateful and very fortunate to be able to spend time with him and hear his teaching. Rinpoche also gave the Refuge Vow ceremony. Many of us took the Refuge Vow with him, including Joy and me. Those of us who took refuge became the founding members of what would become the Gainesville Karma Thegsum Choling Center for Buddhist Studies.

That was my introduction to Rinpoche and his kindness and compassion for beings. Our center has continued to grow from that beginning. For nearly forty years, I have continued to return to KTD for teachings many times. Over those years, I also had the good fortune to travel with Rinpoche to various places, including, the Wutai Mountains in China and many other sacred places in India, Nepal, and Tibet. He provided so many opportunities for those of us who traveled with him that would not have been available to us traveling alone. With Rinpoche, special places became available, and meetings with remarkable people occurred frequently. We found ourselves in incredible situations, meeting with masters such as His Holiness Karmapa, Tai Situ Rinpoche, and Traleg Kyabgon Rinpoche.

In 2008, we traveled with Rinpoche to Namo Buddha Monastery in Nepal where I received the Gelong vows with Khenchen Thrangu Rinpoche.

We also went to the Kagyu Monlam in Bodhgaya, India, led by Karmapa. The last Kagyu Monlam I attended in India was in 2016, when His Holiness Karmapa gave Rinpoche special recognition, honoring his life, and made long-life prayers for him. Those were wonderful and memorable events.

Most of the time spent with Rinpoche was attending teachings, having interviews, and for empowerments and pujas. These were all part of my training. Hearing, contemplating, and practicing are the three essential points for a practitioner. We hear the teaching first, then contemplate what we have heard, and if there are questions, we consult the guru for clarification to practice correctly. Rinpoche's wisdom and skillful ways of resolving our problems were always very helpful. This was particularly evident in our Board-of-Trustee meetings at KTD. He would resolve complicated issues with insight and kindness.

We continued our teacher-student relationship until his passing at the age of ninety-six, on October 6, 2019. Even after his passing, I still strongly feel his presence in my life. I feel his presence every day. My confidence in him continued to develop over time. He never contradicted his genuine kindness, either with me or with anyone else that I had seen him with. I am sure everyone that you interview will talk about his kindness. Everything reinforced that initial feeling I had when I first met him. From his compassion and caring for that little green tree frog to his caring for the many students and seekers who came to see him over many years, he showed loving-kindness and compassion for all beings.

Interviewer: Tell us how you came to do the three-year retreat with Khenpo Rinpoche and what was that like for you.

As my study and learning went deeper, it became clear that it was necessary for me to do the three-year retreat at Karme Ling. As we know, life is short. He always taught us that we have to take responsibility for our actions in this lifetime, and we don't want to waste this precious human birth that is so difficult to acquire and so easily lost.

My qualifications for the retreat were not that good. I was an Acupuncture Physician with a busy practice and the founder, director, and primary teacher at The Florida School of Acupuncture and Oriental Medicine. I was also happily married to my wife Joy and a householder with many responsibilities. Joy was aware that an important endeavor for me in this life was to do the three-year retreat with Rinpoche at Karme Ling. This would be a major shift in our lives. Three years away from each other is a long time and would not be easy. Not very many relationships survive that stress. But she understood my aspiration and was always supportive.

Then in the mid-1990s, Rinpoche's health declined. It was rumored that the next retreat, the third retreat at Karme Ling, might be the last one that he would preside over. It was now or never since I wanted to do the retreat under his guidance. When I presented my aspiration to Joy, she was wonderful. She suggested I call Rinpoche and ask if I could join the next retreat starting in just a few weeks. When I called, the retreat manager, Karma Lodro, answered the phone and said that Rinpoche was right there beside him. I thought that this was very auspicious! I asked my question, "Would Rinpoche accept me into the next retreat?" His answer came immediately, "Yes," and with one additional comment, "Study Tibetan!"

In our retreat, Lama Karma, Lama Tsultrim, Lama Tarchin, and Lama Zopa, along with two other men who did not pursue post-retreat activities as lamas, were also in retreat with me. The lamas mentioned above were more experienced and a great help to me. It was a time of concentrated practice with a rigorous schedule. Rinpoche would generally have breakfast with us in the morning. During our breakfast together, Lama Karma was gathering stories from Rinpoche's time in Tibet as a young man and of the many Siddhas he had met over the years. These stories would become the book *Siddhas of Ga* (see bibliography). We were all very fortunate to hear these stories as Rinpoche was telling them around our breakfast table. This was another example of Rinpoche's skillful means. He knew that hearing the stories about the lives of these great practitioners would provide added inspiration for us to make the most of our time in retreat. Lama Karma's book is available, you may find it inspirational too!

Doing the three-year retreat gave me tools to work with for the rest of my life. Having the good fortune of being in retreat, with Rinpoche as our guide and mentor, and doing the internal practices of the three-year retreat only increased my confidence and devotion. It is essential to have confidence in the teaching, in the teacher, in the path, and in the fruition. As is said in our *Mahamudra* Lineage Prayer, "Devotion is the head of meditation, as is taught." With Rinpoche, it was easy.

Interviewer: What happened after retreat?

Near the end of the retreat, I asked Rinpoche what he would like me to do after retreat. He asked me to return to Florida to teach and guide the Dharma Centers in Florida, which I have continued to do.

Being the Lama and Spiritual Director for the Florida Dharma Centers has been a blessing for me. For over thirty-five years, I have been offering teachings and guiding students. As a result, many people have come to the Dharma Centers to learn and practice Buddhadharma. Following Rinpoche's wishes, in addition to Gainesville, I also provide assistance to Jacksonville KTC, also founded by Khenpo Karthar Rinpoche around the same time as Gainesville KTC in 1987. I also provide guidance and support to the Amelia Island KKSG. I have felt Rinpoche's blessing and guidance every step of the way.

Rinpoche changed my life in many ways. As another example, he appointed me as a member of the Board of Trustees of KTD. I am grateful for his trust and confidence in my capacity to serve KTD and Karmapa. I felt honored in being able to serve Karmapa and Rinpoche in that way.

Interviewer: Is language a hindrance for people to study Tibetan Buddhism in the centers?

It is not a hindrance. My Tibetan has never been good, so I probably use more English than many other lamas do. In our center, we have our practices in English and Tibetan. The original Tibetan text does have a special blessing, and it does have a nice tune for chanting, but knowing and embodying the words are very important. As Tibetan Buddhism becomes more popular in the West, it will make a transition, and it is important for people to have a heartfelt connection with the words and the meaning. For most, a foreign language is a difficult way to do that.

Karmapa is making changes to previous translations of the texts and prayers to better convey the essential meaning. I use English translations in my practice, in my teaching, and in prayers that we use in the center.

Interviewer: Do you have challenges in work and life?

Definitely. We live in a samsaric world, there are always challenges. This is the Buddha's First Noble Truth. It is important to know the essence of suffering as this leads to understanding its cause. We must cultivate the right view.

In 2018, I attended the 9th North American Monlam in New York with Rinpoche. Karmapa was presiding. It was the morning of the final day of the teachings. The Sangha members and lay practitioners were taking their seats, and we were about to begin the morning session. Karmapa entered and took his seat on the throne to begin the morning prayers. My seat was with the ordained Sangha and was close to Karmapa. As I was getting ready to take my seat, I fell down with a massive stroke. I had lost all control of my right side and lost the ability to move my right arm or hand or my right leg. I could not move a finger or a toe. As I collapsed, the person next to me asked if I was okay. I remember getting the words out, "I'm having a stroke." He and several other monks immediately carried me out to an ambulance waiting just outside. It was quite a scene. Fortunately, because it was such a large gathering, there was medical support, and an ambulance was waiting for such an emergency.

This happened in front of Karmapa, Khenpo Rinpoche, and all the other Rinpoches, Khenpos, Lamas, monks, and nuns from all over the world. I was taken to Lenox Hill Hospital in Manhattan, which is an excellent hospital for stroke. I was taken good care of there. But the doctors couldn't give me any prognosis. My worry was that I would be permanently paralyzed and become wheelchair bound.

The next day Rinpoche came to visit me in the hospital, along with Khenpo Ugyen and Lama Karma. Out of his immense compassion and caring, he came to my hospital room. I was so happy to see them. Rinpoche said that Karmapa had asked about me. Rinpoche had done the Mo divination about my condition and future outcome. He told me not to worry and that I was going to be fine. He said I would completely recover. Khenpo Ugyen said too he was doing the Medicine Buddha practice for me, and I should do the same. The Medicine Buddha practice has been a practice I had been doing daily for years, and I would certainly continue to do so. At that point, my worries went away. I had such trust and confidence in Rinpoche and the Dharma. I feel this must have greatly facilitated my healing.

It happened that my recovery was very rapid. And I'm perfectly fine now, without any remaining disability. The physicians and those who were taking care of me said they hadn't seen a recovery like this for a stroke as massive as I had.

I am sure with all the prayers of those at Monlam, Karmapa's blessing, and Rinpoche's reassurance and doing the MO divination and the many prayers being offered on my behalf made this remarkable recovery possible. One person called it my "stroke of luck."

As it turned out, that visit with Rinpoche in the hospital was the last time I really had personal time with him.

Interviewer: Do you believe in miracles?

There are events that would be called miraculous. We have the mention of miracles in all religious traditions. In a way, being born human with all the advantages and qualities we have to practice Dharma is a miracle. In the sutras we find many references to the Buddha performing miracles in his life. Reading the life of the Buddha is highly recommended.

It is a difficult time for so many. When we look around the world, we see the constant strife, turmoil, stress, and so on. I know a lot of people do practice to reduce the stress of modern life, for better health, better sleep or to lower blood pressure, etc. But the clear point that I got from Rinpoche is we're practicing for liberation. We're doing our practice for one thing and one thing only—that is to attain Buddhahood for the benefit for oneself and for others. It is a miracle that one can encounter the Dharma and then have the causes and conditions necessary to pursue this precious opportunity and work diligently with clarity and discipline toward that goal every day. It is a miracle to find a role model these days that lives up to this task. Rinpoche did that!

There's a very small percentage of people who actually practice Dharma and who have the good fortune to come into contact with an authentic teacher who can guide them in this pursuit of Buddhahood. Rinpoche's students are very fortunate to have found an authentic teacher as skilled in the Dharma as Rinpoche. However, three years is a drop in the bucket, if we look from the perspective of beginningless time. The time in retreat has given me a solid foundation from which to confidently practice. This is very important.

Rinpoche has patiently guided his many students, giving them the necessary instruction and skills in knowing how to practice. Indeed, to find a teacher and learn how to practice the dharma in this crazy upside-down world can be seen as another miracle that Rinpoche has facilitated.

We have the good karma to have this opportunity to be connected with a spiritual master in this life. One who can guide us in such a profound way, is a miracle. Generally, it is not easy to have confidence in a teacher, but in Rinpoche, trust and confidence arose easily and spontaneously. And he never contradicted that confidence from the first day I met him to the present.

We were so fortunate to be his students. This kind of teacher is hard to come by. To have the good fortune to be connected with a holder of the lineage such as Rinpoche and to receive his blessing is truly another miracle. I pray every day that until enlightenment is reached, may I never be separated from my precious teacher.

Interviewer: Is there any difference between His Holiness Karmapa and Rinpoche?

Having had the opportunity to be in retreat with Rinpoche, I was able to see him more frequently. He is my *Tsa-way Lama* (root guru). He is the one who opened my eyes.

Karmapa is the head of our lineage. I feel his blessing as well. I've had the good fortune of having time with him too as a member of the KTD Board of Trustees and at his residence in India. Once at his residence in India, while I was seeing patients, Karmapa came in and said, "I do Tai Chi, too."

I was so amazed. We had never talked about that, but he knew that I taught Tai Chi. He then proceeded to do a little of the Tai Chi form! At that moment, I felt he knew everything about me, and at the same time, I felt his love and compassion. That experience had a big impact on me.

We are very blessed. Karmapas aren't always here, the teachings of the Buddha aren't always here. We have the good fortune of being at a time right now, where the Buddha's teaching is available, and we have wonderful teachers. To have Karmapa present, teach, and be available to us is such a blessing. We are fortunate to have that connection with our lineage masters, the sources of light for us all. Rinpoche's love and devotion for his teacher, the Gyalwa Karmapa, was exemplary. He always led by example.

Interviewer: How was Rinpoche's passing for you personally?

Even Rinpoche's passing was an act of loving-kindness and compassion. His timing was perfect. I have the feeling he knew that the pandemic was coming, that there would be a lockdown at KTD, and things would stop. He chose the time that we could all come to his funeral and a time when Vajra Master Lama Tobden from Thrangu Monastery just happened to be at KTD, giving a special reading transmission of Karma Chagme's collected works. This reading transmission was also important to Rinpoche, and it was successfully completed just before Rinpoche's passing. Lama Tobden was able to stay after Rinpoche's passing to help lead the ceremonies, including Rinpoche's cremation at Karme Ling. It was such a blessing for all of us to be together and do the pujas at Karme Ling and be a part of his passing in such a memorable way. In retrospect, the timing of Rinpoche's passing could not have been more perfect.

When we lose our teacher, it is certainly natural to feel a great loss, and I do miss seeing him. However, I don't feel the loss of his presence in my life or in my practice. I still feel his presence every day. When I do my practice, he is with me, just as present as ever. Although I miss the days when I could see him at KTD, I still feel like he is here with me.

I pray daily for his quick and auspicious rebirth and to see him again in this very life! My daily prayer includes the aspiration that until enlightenment is reached, may we always be together.

I feel very fortunate to be one of Rinpoche's students. When we think about the qualities of the spiritual master, it has to be someone who is available, not necessarily living in the same area, but who you feel a connection with. I'm fortunate to have found that with Khenpo

Karthar Rinpoche. As I said, it's hard to find role models in this world. And Rinpoche was always a role model for me, in his kindness, his work ethic, and so on. He worked tirelessly, teaching, having interviews with students, sewing Dharma materials, consecrating statues, and taking care of the monastery. He was there with me when I received the Getsul vows and also some years later in Nepal, when receiving the Gelong ordination and he presented me with the robes I would wear as a monk.

My ordination name is Karma Lodro Sangpo, which means "excellent intelligence." However, Rinpoche always called me Losang, a contraction of the name and translated it as "kind-hearted." These are some of the wonderful memories I have of him. He certainly felt like my spiritual father. There are many things I am so grateful for.

(Interviewer interjects; tears came to Lama Losang's eyes as he talks about this.)

He communicated his care and love in all those ways. Every time I think about his kindness, tears come. Another precious memory was his blessing and preparation of the central Medicine Buddha statue in the shrine room of our Gainesville KTC. I was given a large Medicine Buddha statue by a donor. I sent it to Rinpoche to fill and bless. Not only did he do that, but he had the Buddha painted in gold! In addition, he had a beautiful throne constructed for it to sit on. He had the throne painted and then personally decorated it with beautiful ornaments and colorful stones.

Figure 7: Medicine Buddha at Gainesville KTC; Hand-Decorated by Khenpo Karthar Rinpoche

He has been like a spiritual father to me. My biological father taught me the ways of the world. He did not give me instructions on how to attain Buddhahood. It was from Rinpoche that I learned a different way of being. Instead of pursuing the mundane accomplishments of a samsaric life, Rinpoche pointed me in the direction of Buddhahood. He set me firmly on the path to liberation and has guided me ever since.

Rinpoche opened my heart in a way that no one else has. He taught me things that no one else could. Hopefully, I am living and practicing in a way that will benefit as many people as possible, through teaching and inspiration. If I can be a source of inspiration to others, like Rinpoche was to me, I think that would make him very happy.

As I'm looking at the camera now and doing this interview, I have a picture of Rinpoche in front of me. I'm looking at Rinpoche and feeling like we're doing this together.

This life is fleeting. I've been blessed to have lived seventy-four years, but none of us know how many more years we might have. I am thankful and happy to be able to practice what Rinpoche has taught me.

Interviewer: Lama, please stay a long time with us.

That's my intention. I pray for a long life to be able to benefit others and to study and practice until enlightenment is reached.

APPENDIX D

Guidelines for Daily Practice

What follows is a brief outline for our daily practice and how to create a sacred space for meditation. This will help provide the proper environment conducive to establishing a meditative mind. Here are some guidelines to follow:

1. Do three prostrations. In many traditions, it is common to perform three prostrations upon entering a shrine room or temple. This practice is rooted in the idea of showing respect, humility, and devotion to the Buddha, the Dharma, and the Sangha.

2. Open your shrine by making an offering of incense, flowers, or lighting a candle. Shrines can have a variety of offerings, depending upon the tradition, culture, and personal preferences of the practitioner. These practices, when done mindfully, are a great source of merit. It is part of our mind-training in the cultivation of virtue.

3. Take your seat and bring to mind the wish to benefit all beings as the motivation for your practice.

4. Contemplate the four thoughts that turn the mind to Dharma:

    a. This precious human birth.
    b. Impermanence.

       c.   Karma.

       d.   Samsara.

5.   Practice *Shamatha* meditation. Begin with mindfully taking twenty-one breaths for twenty-one days. After twenty-one days, you can gradually let go of the counting and extend your meditation time. As your mind becomes increasingly stable, add *Vipashyana* and rest in the undisturbed meditative absorption in the lucid clarity of your natural mind.

6.   Contemplate the Four Immeasurables:

       a.   Love – May all beings be happy and have the causes of happiness.

       b.   Compassion – May all beings be free of suffering and the causes of suffering.

       c.   Sympathetic Joy – May all beings never be separated from the great bliss that is free from suffering.

       d.   Equanimity – May all beings rest in equanimity, free from attachment and aversion, having the same great love for all.

7.   Dedicate the Merit. Engender the motivation to give the merit generated by our practice for the benefit and happiness of all beings.

APPENDIX E

Mala: How to Use Buddhist Prayer Beads

Mala is a Sanskrit word for the prayer beads used for counting mantra recitations. It is used like a rosary as found in other religious traditions. They are commonly seen in all Tibetan Buddhist communities, worn around the wrists, around the neck, or dangling from the fingers of a practitioner reciting mantras. Practitioners repeat, mentally or out loud, a variety of mantras thousands or even hundreds of thousands of times.

A *mala* is generally a string of 108 beads made of crystal, precious or semiprecious stones, like lapis lazuli (often used for Medicine Buddha practice), wood (like sandalwood), and seeds (like bodhi seed or lotus seed). Bodhi-seed *mala*s are considered good for all practices.

Your *mala* is a tool for your practice, and it is not worn as jewelry. However, you will see special stones, like turquoise or coral, on a *mala* to mark an interval of twenty-seven beads that indicates you are a quarter of the way through. These added beads are "extra" and increase the total bead count to 111, instead of 108.

Each time you work your way around the *mala*, you are considered to have completed one hundred mantra recitations. The added "extra" beads are to make up for any distractions, miscounting, or mistakes you may have made along the way. There are also wrist malas with twenty-seven beads.

These are sometimes used for counting prostrations when doing *ngondro* and repeated four times for a total of 108. Even if you're not actively counting repetitions of a mantra, proceeding bead by bead through the mala serves to focus and calm the mind.

There is also one larger bead, sometimes called a "guru bead." This is considered to have special significance, representing one's guru. But from a practical point of view, it is the starting point of the circuit and is not counted among the 108 total. Some practitioners reverse the mala and go back the other direction when arriving at the guru bead and don't cross over it. There are no strict rules when it comes to *malas*. As with most things in Buddhism, what matters most is your intention and your attitude of devotion and *bodhichitta*.

We begin with the first bead next to the guru bead. Hold the bead between the index finger and the thumb, recite your mantra, out loud or silently, then move to the next bead with a rolling motion of your thumb and continue to repeat your mantra until you get to the guru bead. You have now completed one hundred mantras. Most practitioners do not pass over the guru bead but instead reverse the direction by turning the mala around and starting a new circuit of one hundred, going back the way they came. It is another skillful means to cultivate mindfulness. Some say that if you continue in the same direction crossing over the guru bead, it is like stepping over your Lama!

When counting high numbers of mantra recitations, as in yidam practice or ngondro, it is helpful to have counters on your mala. Many use two shorter strings with ten small beads with a miniature dorje on the end of one and a miniature bell attached to the end of the other string. The dorje and bell are the most commonly used sacred ritual objects, and these images are frequently used on the ends of counters. These are placed about six to nine beads on either side of the guru bead, but you can place where you like on the *mala*. The *dorje* counter keeps count of each one hundred mantra repetitions; that is one full mala. After completion of each *mala* mantra repetition, move one bead forward on the *dorje* counter. After ten complete mala repetitions, you will have moved all ten beads on the *dorje* counter and have recited one thousand mantras.

Next, after completing one thousand mantras, you will move one counter forward on the bell counter to mark the completion of one thousand mantras completed.

Now move all beads back down on the dorje counter and begin a new count of one hundred. Continue in this way, keeping count of your mantra repetitions; you will be able to count up to ten thousand mantra recitations. If you are counting more than this, record the ten thousand in a notebook and begin the process again.

You might ask, *Why do we use the dorje and bell on our counters?* There is a reason. The dorje, also known as a Vajra, and bell are important ritual objects in Tibetan Buddhism, often used together in various ceremonies and practices.

The dorje represents the indestructible, diamond-like nature of enlightenment and is held in the *right hand* during rituals. It has a symmetrical shape with a central axis and four prongs, representing the Four Immeasurables: compassion, loving-kindness, empathetic joy, and equanimity.

The bell represents wisdom and the feminine principle in Buddhism and is held in the *left hand* during rituals. It has a deep, resonant sound believed to dispel negative energy and purify the environment. The bell is also associated with Prajnaparamita, the female embodiment of wisdom, and is used in combination with the dorje to represent the union of wisdom and compassion. Together, the dorje and bell symbolize the integration of wisdom and compassion, the two essential qualities necessary for spiritual awakening.

Your *mala* is said to grow in spiritual significance the more you use it for mantra recitation. You can have it blessed by your guru, and it is treated with respect. Like other Dharma materials, we wouldn't put it on the floor or put other objects on top of it, throw it, or use it for anything besides our practice.

When we are not using them, malas are usually wrapped around the wrists or hung around the necks, remembering that they are not worn, like a necklace, for decoration. When not in use, you can keep it on your altar.

This is my bodhi-seed mala showing the extra three beads and the additional counters.

Figure 8: Lama Losang's Mala

Bibliography and Recommended Reading

Benson, Herbert. *Beyond the Relaxation Response.* New York, New York: Berkley Publications, 1985.

Bole, David N. *The Effect of the Relaxation Response on the Positive Personality Characteristics of Paraprofessional Counselors.* Gainesville, Florida: University of Florida Press, 1985.

Drodhul, Lama Karma. *Siddha of Ga, Remembered by Khenpo Karthar Rinpoche.* Woodstock, New York, KTD Publications, 2013.

Karmapa Ogyen Trinley Dorje. *Freedom Through Meditation.* Woodstock, New York: KTD Publications, 2018.

Khenpo Karthar Rinpoche. *Karma Chakme's Mountain Dharma.* Vols. 1–4. Woodstock, New York: KTD Publications, 2006.

————. *Dharma Paths.* Ithaca, New York: Snow Lion Publication, 2011.

Kongtrul, Jamgon. *The Great Path of Awakening.* Translated by Ken McLeod. Boston: Shambhala Publications, 1987.

————. *The Torch of Certainty.* Translated by Judith Hanson. Boston: Shambhala Publications, 1977.

—————. *Treasury of Knowledge, Book One: Myriad Worlds*. Kalu Rinpoche Translation Group. Ithaca, New York: Snow Lion Publications, 2003.

Kyabgon, Traleg. *The Essence of Buddhism: An Introduction to Its Philosophy and Practice*. Boston: Shambhala Publications, 2001.

—————. *Mind at Ease: Self-Liberation through* Mahamudra *Meditation*. Boston: Shambhala Publications, 2005.

—————. *ThePractice of Lojong: Cultivating Compassion through Training the Mind*. Boston: Shambhala Publications, 2007.

Miller, Lisa. *The Awakened Brian: The New Science of Spirituality and Our Quest for an Inspired Life*. New York: Random House, 2021.

Thrangu Rinpoche. *Medicine Buddha Teachings*. Ithaca, New York: Snow Lion Publications, 2004.

—————. *The Mahamudra Lineage Prayer: A Guide to Practice*. Boulder, Colorado: Snow Lion Publications, 2018.

—————. *Essentials of Mahamudra: Looking Directly at the Mind*. Boulder, Colorado: Snow Lion Publications, 2014.

—————. *The Three Vehicles of Buddhist Practice*. Translated by Ken Holmes. Crestone, Colorado: Namo Buddha Publications, 2003.

Dharma Dictionary

Note: "S" stands for Sanskrit, "T" for Tibetan.

abhisheka – See empowerment.

Abhidharma – See Tripitaka.

accumulations – (merit and wisdom) (1) The accumulation of merit is developed through physical and material devotion to the spiritual path and compassionate action to living beings. This creates conditions favorable to enlightenment and results in (2) the accumulation of wisdom, which is the realization gained from meditation practice.

ahimsa – (S. "non-harming") In Buddhism, non-harming of living beings is considered one of the most important aspects of the Buddhist's path. Vegetarianism for monks and nuns in most Buddhist cultures is based on this principle of ahimsa.

Amitabha – (S.; T. Opakme) The Sambhogakaya Buddha of boundless light, red in color and of the Padma family. *See Buddha families.*

amrita – (S.; T. dutsi) The nectar of meditative bliss, also the consecrated liquid used in Vajrayana meditation practices.

arhat – (S.; T. dra-chompa, "foe destroyer") One who has attained the result of the Hinayana path by purifying the conflicting emotions and their causes.

Avalokiteshvara – See Chenrezig.

bardo – (T. "between two") A gap or intermediate state; the intermediate state between death and rebirth. Other bardos include the dream bardo and the meditation bardo.

bhumi – (S.; T. "stage") One of the ten stages of realization on the Bodhisattva path. The first bhumi begins with great joy and the stabilized realization of shunyata.

blessings – (T. chinlab) The experience of bliss that results from one's devotion in opening oneself to the guru in meditation practice.

bliss – (S. sukha; T. dewa) A meditative experience of calm happiness.

bodhichitta – (S.; T. jangchup chi sem, "mind of enlightenment") Relative bodhichitta is the aspiration to develop loving-kindness and compassion and to deliver all sentient beings from samsara. Absolute bodhichitta is actually working to save all beings. According to Gampopa, absolute bodhichitta is shunyata indivisible from compassion—radiant, unshakable, and impossible to formulate with concepts.

Bodhisattva – (S. "awakened being"; T. jangchup sempa, "enlightened mind hero") In one sense, a person who has vowed to attain perfect Buddhahood for the benefit of all beings and who has begun to progress through the ten *bhumis* of the Bodhisattva path. In another sense, a being who has already attained perfect Buddhahood but who, through the power of the Bodhisattva Vow, returns to the world for the benefit of beings.

Bodhisattva Vow – (T. jang-dam) The commitment to work on the Mahayana path for the enlightenment of all beings; this is a vow taken in a formal ceremony in the presence of the guru.

Bodhisattvayana – See Mahayana.

Buddha – (S. "awakened, enlightened"; T. sang-gye, "eliminated negative habitual patterns and perfected all virtue") May refer to the principle of enlightenment or to any enlightened being, in particular to Shakyamuni Buddha, the historical Buddha of our age. A Buddha is called a Victorious One.

Buddha families – (T. sang-gye chi rik) The families of the five Sambhogakaya Buddhas and their five wisdoms. Everything in the world can be expressed in terms of the predominant energy of one of these five families, and all deities in Tibetan iconography are associated with one of the five Buddhas. In samsaric experience, the five wisdoms become translated into the five poisons, which are conflicting emotions. The five families and their corresponding colors, Buddhas, wisdoms, and conflicting emotions are, respectively, (1) white, Buddha, Vairochana, all-pervading wisdom, and ignorance; (2) blue, Vajra, Akshobya, mirror-like wisdom, and aggression; (3) yellow, Ratna, Ratnasambava, wisdom of equanimity, and pride; (4) red, Padma, Amitabha, wisdom of discriminating awareness, and passion; (5) green, Karma, Amoghasiddhi, all-accomplishing wisdom, and envy. (Lists are taken from various sources and may differ slightly.)

Buddha-nature – (S. sugatagarbha; T. deshin shekpa nyingpo) The basic goodness of all beings, the inherent potential within each person to attain complete Buddhahood, regardless of race, gender, or nationality.

Buddhadharma – (S.; T. san-gye chi cho, ten-pay ten-pa) The teachings of the Buddha, often used in preference to the term Buddhism.

chakra – (S.; T. khorlo, "circle, wheel") One of the five primary energy centers of the subtle body, located along the central channel at the crown of the head, throat, heart, navel, and genitals.

Chenrezig – (T.; S. Avalokiteshvara) The Bodhisattva of compassion, the union or essence of compassion of all the Buddhas. His Holiness the 16th Gyalwa Karmapa was believed to be an emanation of Chenrezig, as is His Holiness the Dalai Lama.

co-emergent wisdom – (S. sahajajnana; T. lhan cig skyes pai yeshe) The simultaneous arising of samsara and nirvana, giving birth to wisdom.

compassion – (S. karma; T. nying je) The motivation and action of a Bodhisattva and the guiding principle of the Mahayana path. Compassion arises from experiencing the suffering of oneself and others or from relinquishing one's attachment to samsara, or it may develop spontaneously from the recognition of shunyata.

conflicting emotions – See poisons.

dakini – (S.; T. khandroma, "space walker") A wrathful or semi-wrathful female yidam, signifying the feminine energy principle. The dakini are crafty and playful, representing the basic space of fertility out of which samsara and nirvana arise. They inspire the union of skillful means and wisdom. More generally, a dakini can be a type of messenger or protector. A daka is the male counterpart to a dakini.

damaru – (S.) A small hand drum, usually two-headed, made of either skulls or wood and used frequently in Vajrayana practice.

dark age – The present-world age, characterized by degraded society, warfare, perverted views, and lack of faith in spirituality, including the degeneration of all discipline, morality, and wisdom.

Dedicate the Merit – Dedicating the Merit of our practice is a way of cultivating *bodhichitta* by extending any virtuous activity for the benefit of others.

Dewachen – (T.; S. Sukhavati; "Great Bliss") The Western Pure Land of Buddha Amitabha. One can practice meditation and achieve enlightenment in the pure lands without danger of falling into the cycle of samsara, not to be confused with heaven or the realm of the gods, which, in Buddhism, is considered to be only a materialistic paradise.

Dharma – (S.; T. cho, "truth, law") There are thirteen different meanings altogether for the word Dharma. It can refer to the ultimate truth, the Buddha's teaching, or the law governing all existence.

dharmachakra – (S.; T. cho chi khorlo, "Wheel of Dharma") Generally, this term is used in expressions such as dharmachakra pravartana ("turning the Wheel of Dharma"), which refers to teaching the Dharma. More technically, it can refer to the heart chakra.

dharmadhatu – (S.; T. cho-ying, "sphere of Dharma") The all-encompassing space or unconditional totality, unoriginating and unchanging, in which all phenomena arise, dwell, and cease.

Dharmakaya – (S.; T. choku, "body of truth") Enlightenment itself, wisdom beyond any reference point—unoriginated, primordial mind, devoid of content. See trikaya.

dharmapala – (S.; T. cho chong, "protector of the Dharma") A type of deity that protects the practitioner from deceptions and obstacles. Although usually wrathful, the dharmapala are compassionate, performing the enlightened actions of pacifying, enriching, magnetizing, and destroying, thus protecting the integrity of the teachings and practice.

dharmata – (S.; T. cho-nyi, "Dharma itself") The essence of reality, completely pure nature.

doha – (S.) A verse or song spontaneously composed by Vajrayana practitioners as an expression of their realization, as for example the Dharma songs collected in the Rain of Wisdom.

Dorje Chang – See Vajradhara.

elements – (T. jungwa) According to the Abhidharma, all materiality can be seen as having the qualities of one of the four elements: earth, water, fire, and air.

empowerment – (S. abhisheka; T. wangkur) An initiation conferred privately or to groups enabling those who receive it to practice a particular meditation or yogic method under a qualified spiritual master.

emptiness – See shunyata.

enlightenment – (T. jangchup) Jang refers to the total purification of the two obscurations, and chup refers to perfected wisdom that encompasses relative and ultimate truths.

five skandhas – (S.; T. pungpo, "aggregates" or "heaps") The five skandhas are the psychological aggregates that make up the personality of the individual and his or her experiences. They are form, feeling, perception, formation, and consciousness. In Vajrayana, the skandhas correspond to the five Buddha potentials.

Four Immeasurables – (S. apramana; T. tse-me shi) A prayer recited especially during ngondro practice. Maitri is loving-kindness, the wish that all beings have happiness and the cause of happiness. Karuna is compassion, the wish that all beings be free from suffering and the causes of suffering. Mudita is great joy, the wish that all beings never be separated from the great bliss that is free from all suffering. Upeksha is equanimity, the wish that all beings dwell in the great impartiality that is free from all attraction and aversion.

Four Noble Truths – (T. pakpay denpa shi) The truths that unenlightened existence is permeated by suffering, that the cause of suffering is delusion operating through dualistic clinging and the resulting emotional and karmic patterns, that an experience beyond suffering is possible, and that there is a path that can lead beings to the experience of the cessation of suffering.

Gelug – (T.) The order of Tibetan Buddhism founded by Tsong Khapa (1357–1419). Gelug refers to the teachings of this lineage and Gelugpa to its practitioners.

Ghanta – (T. drilbu) Bell used with Vajra (dorje) in tantric rituals.

Guru Rinpoche – Guru Padmasambhava, also known as the "Lotus-Born"; with Atisa, responsible for the "second spreading" of the Dharma in Tibet.

guru – Religious teacher, also called spiritual friend. See roots, three.

guru yoga – Last of the four special foundations or ngondro practices.

Gyalwa – A title meaning "victorious," as in Gyalwa Karmapa.

Hinayana – (S.; T. tek-chung, tek-men, "lesser vehicle") The first of the Three Yanas, which is subdivided into the Shravakayana and Pratyekabuddhayana. The aim of Hinayana practice is personal liberation from suffering.

impermanence – (S. anitya; T. mitakpa) The doctrine that the material world is characterized by constant change and the nonexistence of phenomena.

interdependence – (T. tendrel) The doctrine that all phenomena are related in their appearance and manifestation. No event arises that is not related to all other events.

Jetsun – (T. "revered") An honorific term applied to great teachers.

jnana – (S.; T. yeshe, "primordial knowing") Discriminating awareness wisdom that transcends all dualistic conception.

Kagyu – (T. abbreviation for ka shi gyupa) One of the four main lineages of Tibetan Buddhism originating with Vajradhara Buddha and transmitted to the Indian master Tilopa. It was then transmitted in succession to Naropa, Marpa, Milarepa, and Gampopa. It is also called the practice lineage because of its emphasis on direct experiential practice and intuitive understanding of the teachings. There are four main subsects of the Kagyu lineage, the largest being the Karma Kagyu—the lineage founded by Dusum Khyenpa, the First Gyalwa Karmapa, who was a disciple of Gampopa.

kalpa – (T.) An extremely long period, sometimes estimated at 4.320 million years.

Kangyur – (T.) Tantric teachings of the Buddha.

kapala – (S.; T. topa, "skull cup") A symbolic implement used in Vajrayana practices.

karma – (S. "action") The doctrine of cause and result, which states one's present experience is a product of previous actions and volitions, and future conditions depend on one's present conduct.

Karmapa – (T. trin-le-pa, "activity") The head of the Karma Kagyu sect of Tibetan Buddhism, a fully enlightened Bodhisattva and an emanation of Avalokiteshvara. Historically, the first line of recognized reincarnating lamas, now celebrating over 900 years, of which Dusum Khyenpa was the first. Ogyen Trinley Dorje is now the 17th Karmapa.

Kham – A province in Eastern Tibet where the Kagyu lineage enjoyed great popularity.

khatak – (T.) A long white scarf, customarily presented in Tibet as a sign of salutation and respect.

Khenpo – (T.) Title of the abbot of a Tibetan monastery or a professor of sacred literature.

klesha – (S.; T. nyonmong, "defilement, delusion") A mental state that produces conflicting emotions and confusion and thus disturbs mental well-being and peace.

Kriya yoga – (S.; T. ja-gyu) The first tantric Yana, which emphasizes purity and the understanding that all phenomena are inherently pure and sacred. The deities are visualized as external and transparent, and the practitioner emphasizes purification and ritual action.

Lama – (T; S. guru) A Buddhist teacher of meditation who has completed the traditional three-year, three-month retreat and been given the title or appointment by his or her teacher.

lung – (T. "connection") A transmission blessing in which a master reads through a sadhana or liturgy, usually quite rapidly, thereby empowering the hearers to practice it.

Mahakala – (S.; T. nakpo chenpo, "great black one," or bernakchen, "black-gowned one" (two-armed Mahakala)). Mahakala is the chief dharmapala or wrathful protector of the Dharma. A female Mahakala is Mahakali.

Mahamudra – (S.; T. chak gya chenpo, "great symbol") The great seal or ultimate nature of the mind, which is not stained by the klesha. Another term for enlightenment, Mahamudra refers to the meditative transmission handed down, especially by the Kagyu school, from Vajradhara Buddha to Tilopa and so on in a direct line to the present lineage holders.

Mahayana – (S.; T. tek then, "great vehicle") The second teaching Buddha presented on Vulture Peak Mountain, where he emphasized the importance of uniting compassion and wisdom.

Maitreya – (S.; T. jampa) The coming Buddha; in other words, the Buddha who will appear next after Shakyamuni in this present kalpa or age. Maitreya Buddha will not appear for tens of thousands of years.

mala – (S.; T. trengwa) Buddhist prayer beads similar to a rosary; usually strung with 108 beads.

mandala – (S.; T. chilkhor, "center and periphery") Arrangement of deities or their emblems, usually in the form of a circle, representing a pattern, structure, or group. Mandalas may be painted, made of colored sand or heaps of rice, or represented by three-dimensional models.

Manjushri – (S.; T. Jampalyang, "gentle and glorious") One of the chief Bodhisattvas, Manjushri is depicted with a sword and a book. The sword represents prajna. He is known as the Bodhisattva of Knowledge and Wisdom.

mantra – (S.; T. ngak) Mantra is explained in the tantras as that which protects the cohesiveness of the Vajra mind. It is a means of transforming energy through sound, expressed by speech, breathing, and movement. Mantra is usually done in conjunction with visualization and mudra, according to the prescriptions of a sadhana transmitted by one's guru. Mantras are composed of Sanskrit words or syllables expressing the essence, quality, or power of a specific deity.

Mantrayana – See Vajrayana.

Mara – (S; T. du, "devil") The tempter of Shakyamuni Buddha, who appeared just prior to his attaining enlightenment. The Mara include misunderstanding the five skandha as self, being overpowered by conflicting emotions, death, and seduction by the bliss of meditation. Thus, Mara are difficulties the practitioner may encounter.

mudra – (S.; T. chak gya, "sign, symbol, gesture") A mudra may be any sort of symbol. Specifically, mudras are symbolic hand gestures that accompany sadhana practices.

namo – (T. "homage") Often used in the beginning of a song or prayer to pay homage to a Buddha, deity, or teacher.

ngondro – (T. "preliminary") The four foundations or preliminary practices of Vajrayana Buddhism. They consist of refuge and prostrations, Vajrasattva's mantra, mandala offerings, and guru yoga.

Nirmanakaya – (S.; T. tulku, "emanation body") The Buddha who takes form in a physical body. See trikaya.

nirvana – (S.; T. nya ngen le depa, "gone beyond suffering") According to the Hinayana tradition, nirvana means the cessation of ignorance and of conflicting emotions and, therefore, freedom from compulsive rebirth in samsaric suffering. According to the Mahayana tradition, this Hinayana nirvana is only a way station. Complete enlightenment requires not only the cessation of ignorance but also the compassion and skillful means to work with the bewilderment of all sentient beings.

Nyingma – (T. "ancient ones") One of the four major schools of Tibetan Buddhism. The original form of Vajrayana Buddhism brought to Tibet in the eighth century by Padmasambhava (Guru Rinpoche) and others. Practitioners are called Nyingmapas.

path – (T. lam) The practitioner's way to enlightenment.

pecha – (T.) Text.

poisons – (T. duk) Conflicting emotions. The three root poisons are attachment, anger, and ignorance. The five poisons also include pride and jealousy, and the six poisons include also greed.

Practice Lineage – (T. drup-gyu) A name for the Kagyu lineage, which emphasizes its strong allegiance to meditation practice.

prajna – (S.; T. sherab, "knowledge") The ordinary sharpness of awareness that sees, discriminates, and also sees through conceptual discrimination.

Prajnaparamita – (S.; T. sherab chi parol tu chinpa, "Perfection of Knowledge") The Sixth Perfection (Sixth Paramita). Without prajna, the other five transcendent actions would be impure.

puja – See sadhana.

realization – (T. tokpa) The fruition of the path, the attainment of enlightenment or of a particular higher practice.

refuge – (T. chap-dro) By taking the Refuge Vow, one formally becomes a Buddhist. One takes refuge in the triple gem—Buddha as goal, Dharma as path, and Sangha as guide along the path.

Rinpoche – (T. "precious") A title used with the name of a high lama or as a form of address to him.

root guru – (T. tsaway lama) One's main guru and the source of blessings.

sadhana – (S.; T. choga, "liturgy") A type of Vajrayana ritual text, describing the visualization and worship of a deity; the actual meditation practice it sets out.

Sakya – One of the four main schools of Tibetan Buddhism.

samadhi – (S.; T. Ling-ngeie-dzin, "fixing the mind, meditative absorption") A state of total involvement in which the mind rests unwaveringly.

Samantabhadra – (S.; T. Kuntu Zangpo, "all good") The primordial Dharmakaya Buddha, blue in color and naked, often depicted in consort with Kuntu Zangmo, who is white in color.

samaya – (T. dam-tsik, "sacred words") The sacred vow that binds the practitioner to his or her practice and lama.

Sambhogakaya – (S.; T. longku, "enjoyment body") The environment of compassion and communication. The visionary and communicative aspect of Dharmakaya.

samsara – (S.; T. khorwa, "circumambulating") In contrast to nirvana, samsara is the vicious cycle of transmigratory existence, characterized by suffering. It arises out of inability to purify oneself of the six conflicting emotions.

Sangha – (S.; T. gendun, "the virtuous ones") The ordinary Sangha are all the practitioners of Buddhism, and the exalted Sangha are those who are liberated from samsara.

Shakyamuni – (T. Shakya-tuppa) The historical Buddha. Shakya is a clan of ancient India, and Shakyamuni means "sage of the Shakyas."

Shamatha – (S.; T. shinay, "peaceful abiding") A basic meditation practice common to most schools of Buddhism. Its aim is to quiet the mind and focus it free from distraction. It lays the foundation for Vipashyana.

shunyata – (S.; T. tongpa nyi, "emptiness") A doctrine emphasized in Mahayana that stresses all phenomena are devoid of inherent, concrete existence.

siddhi – (S.; T. ngodrup, "accomplishment") Blessings or accomplishments. The ordinary siddhi involve mastery over the phenomenal world. Supreme siddhi is enlightenment.

Six Perfections – (S. Paramitas; T. parol tu chinpa, "gone to the other side") The main practices of the Mahayana; they are generosity, moral conduct, patience, exertion, meditation or concentration, and insight. They are called "gone to the other side" because through the non-dualistic mind, they transcend karmic entanglements of conventional virtue.

six realms – (T. rikdruk) All samsaric beings belong to one of the six realms. The higher realms are those of the gods, demigods, and humans. The lower realms are those of animals, hungry ghosts, and hell beings. In each realm, there is a typical psychosocial pattern of recreating experience based on one of the six klesha (pride, jealousy, attachment, ignorance, greed, or anger).

stupa – (S.; T. choten) Originally, a memorial mound containing the relics of the Buddha, symbolizing the mind of the Buddha, the Dharmakaya. Later the relics of other enlightened beings, scripture, statues, and so on were included in stupas. Choten means the objects of veneration, ranging from simple altar pieces to very large structures that may be seen for miles around.

Sugatagarbha – (S.; T. deshek nyingpo) Buddha-nature as it manifests on the path.

sutra – (T. do) See Tripitaka.

Svabhavikakaya – (S.; T. ngo-wo nyid-kyi-ku) The essential body of intrinsic nature that encompasses and transcends the three kaya. See trikaya.

tantra – (S.; T. gyud) Continuity; refers to continuity throughout the ground, path, and fruition of the journey. For the practitioner, this means that body, speech, and mind, in all their confused and wakeful manifestations, are included in the path. Tantra specifically refers to the root texts of the Vajrayana and the system of meditation they describe.

Tara – (S. "savioress"; T. Drolma, "liberator lady") An emanation of Avalokiteshvara, Tara is said to have arisen from one of his tears. Embodying female enlightenment and the feminine aspect of compassion, she removes fears and obstacles and is a very popular deity in Tibet. Her two common iconographic forms are white and green.

tashi delek – (T. "May all be auspiciously well") An all-purpose greeting used on holidays and special occasions.

Tathagata – (S.; T. dezhin-shekpa) Synonymous with "Buddha," used especially for the five Sambhogakaya Buddhas.

tendrel – (T.) Dependent and connected. Refers to interdependence, dependent origination, or the Buddhist Law of Causation.

Three Gates – (T. go-sum) Body, speech, and mind; the three modes through which one relates to the phenomenal world.

Three Jewels – (S. Triratna; T. konchok sum) Buddha, Dharma, and Sangha—the three objects of refuge. Buddha is an example of a human being who transcended confusion and also refers to enlightenment itself. Dharma includes the teachings told and written, as well as their realization—the Dharma that is experienced. Sangha is the community of practitioners and also the assemblage of realized ones.

three roots – (T. tsa-wa sum) Guru, yidam, and protector.

torma – (T.; S. bali) A sculpture often made out of flour and molded butter, used as a shrine offering, a feast offering substance, or a representation of deities.

trikaya – (S.; T. kusum, "three bodies") The three aspects of Buddhahood: Dharmakaya, Sambhogakaya, and Nirmanakaya.

Tripitaka – (S. "three baskets") The teachings of Buddha Shakyamuni, later organized into the Vinaya, the sutras, and the Abhidharma. The Vinaya is primarily concerned with monastic discipline or moral conduct; the sutras is usually in the form of dialogues between the Buddha and his disciples, concerning meditation and philosophy; and the Abhidharma contains the higher metaphysical treatises regarding the nature of reality.

triyana – (S.; T. tek-pa sum) Three stages or vehicles of practice.

tsok offering – Blessing and offering of food and drink made in the context of a deity practice.

tulku – (T.; S. Nirmanakaya, "emanation body") An incarnation of a previously realized being.

two obscurations – (T. drippa nyi) (1) Conflicting emotions that obstruct liberation from suffering and (2) fundamental ignorance, primitive beliefs about reality, that obstruct omniscience and right view.

two truths – (T. denpa-nyi) Ultimate truth is emptiness or shunyata. Relative truth belongs to the conventional level of truth. The two truths are inseparable from each other.

upaya – (S.; T. tap, "skillful means") Enlightened beings, through the development of wisdom and the omniscient state of mind, know exactly how, when, and in what form to present the teachings to make them suitable to each individual being without error; an expression of compassion.

Vajra – (S. "adamantine, diamond, indestructible"; T. dorje, "thunderbolt") One of the five Buddha families, the Vajra family is associated with the Buddha Akshobya of the eastern direction. Its quality is pristine clarity and indestructibility. In general, the term Vajra conveys the sense of what is beyond arising and ceasing and hence indestructible. A Vajra is also a ritual scepter used in Vajrayana practice.

Vajradhara – (S.; T. Dorje Chang) The name of the Dharmakaya Buddha. He is depicted as dark blue and is particularly important to the Kagyu lineage, as it is said that Tilopa received Vajrayana teaching directly from Vajradhara.

Vajrasattva – (S.; T. Dorje Sempa) A Buddha of the Vajra family, Vajrasattva is white and is associated with purity. The Vajrasattva mantra is used in many practices, most notably ngondro.

Vajrayana – (S.; T. dorje tekpa, "indestructible vehicle") The vehicle or Yana of tantra. Vajrayana incorporates Hinayana and Mahayana disciplines. See Yana, tantra.

Vidyadhara – Holder of knowledge or insight.

Vinaya – See Tripitaka.

Vipashyana – (S.; T. Lhaktong) Having calmed the mind through Shamatha meditation, the practitioner may begin to have insight into an unimaginable experience of the qualities within one. This clear seeing of the patterns of mind is known as Vipashyana. It expands into wisdom.

Yana – (S.; T. tekpa, "vehicle") The vehicle that carries the practitioner along the path to liberation. In different Yana, the landscapes of the journey, the nature of the practitioner, and the mode of transportation are seen differently. There is a distinctive outlook, practice, action, and fruition in each Yana. The particular Yana presented depends on the evolutionary readiness of the student and the accomplishment of the teacher.

yidam – The Vajrayana practitioner's personal deity that embodies the practitioner's awakened nature. Yidam are Sambhogakaya Buddhas, visualized in accordance with the psychosocial makeup of the practitioner. The student first develops intense devotion toward the guru. This relationship makes it possible for the student to experience intuitive kinship with the lineage and then with the yidam. Identifying with the yidam means the student identifies with his or her own characteristic expression of Buddha-nature, free of distortions. Through seeing one's basic nature in this universalized way, all aspects of it are transmuted into the wisdom of the spiritual path. This leads directly to compassionate action—skillful and lucid.

yoga – (S.; T. naljor) A psychophysical method of spiritual development, concerned with the direction of energy and consciousness. A method to release the intuitive knowledge latent in the heart by learning to control the dispersive tendencies of mind and body.

yogi/yogini – (S.; T. naljorpa/naljorma) A male or female yoga practitioner.

Printed in the United States
by Baker & Taylor Publisher Services